NAILED IT!

THE ESSENTIAL GUIDE TO DO IT YOURSELF

Pavilion
An imprint of HarperCollinsPublishers Ltd
1 London Bridge Street
London SE1 9GF

www.harpercollins.co.uk

HarperCollins*Publishers*
Macken House
39/40 Mayor Street Upper,
Dublin 1
D01 C9W8
Ireland

10 9 8 7 6 5 4 3 2 1

First published in Great Britain by Pavilion
An imprint of HarperCollins*Publishers* 2026

Copyright © Pavilion 2026
Text © Laura Deller 2026

Laura Deller asserts the moral right to be identified as the author of this work. A catalogue record of this book is available from the British Library.

ISBN 9780008748548

Publishing Director: Laura Russell
Commissioning Editor: Lucy Smith
Editorial Assistant: Daisy Gudmunsen
Design Manager: Alice Kennedy-Owen
Production Controller: Grace O'Byrne
Copyeditor: Vicki Murrell
Layout Designer: Hannah Naughton
Illustrator: Tatyana Alanis
Proofreaders: Corinne Colvin and Katie Hewett
Indexer: Vanessa Bird

Printed and bound by RRD in China

All rights reserved. No part of this publication may be reproduced, stored in a retrieval system, or transmitted, in any form or by any means, electronic, mechanical, photocopying, recording or otherwise, without the prior written permission of the publishers.

Without limiting the exclusive rights of any author, contributor or the publisher of this publication, any unauthorised use of this publication to train generative artificial intelligence (AI) technologies is expressly prohibited. HarperCollins also exercise their rights under Article 4(3) of the Digital Single Market Directive 2019/790 and expressly reserve this publication from the text and data mining exception.

Great care has been taken to ensure that the information contained in this book is accurate. However, the law concerning building regulations, planning, local bylaws and related matters is neither static nor simple. Depending on which country you live in, your local conditions may mean that some of this information is not appropriate. If in doubt always consult a qualified professional.

All DIY projects are purely at your own risk. The information provided is a guide intended for able-bodied adults, eighteen years of age and over. No provision has been made to meet individual needs or requirements that may be required. We recommend that you satisfy yourself prior to using this information that it is safe for your own particular circumstances and if necessary, to find alternative methods or information. It is very possible to damage your property, create a hazardous condition, or harm or even kill yourself or others.

A book of this nature cannot replace specialist advice in appropriate cases, and therefore no responsibility can be accepted by the Publisher or by the author for any loss or damage caused by reliance upon the accuracy of such information.

For more information visit:
www.harpercollins.co.uk/green

NAILED IT!

THE ESSENTIAL GUIDE TO DO IT YOURSELF

LAURA DELLER
@HOUSEPROJECTUK

PAVILION

INTRODUCTION 06–11
TOOL CLUB 12–25

PREP IT
26–63

BUILD IT
64–117

DECORATE IT
118–163

PANEL IT
164–185

RENT IT
186–197

UPCYCLE IT
198–213

FINAL THOUGHTS 214
CONVERSIONS 216
NOTES 217–219
INDEX 220–223
ACKNOWLEDGEMENTS 224

CONTENTS

MY JOURNEY

FROM DI-WHY? TO DI-FLY!
Firstly, apologies for the 'DI-Fly'! I'm Laura Deller, a 40-something mum, wife, proud Brummie, science teacher, and DIY and home-content creator. The latter role is one that emerged entirely accidentally around 2020, when I opened an Instagram account to find inspiration for my home renovations. The idea was just to scroll, snoop and screenshot pretty pictures (do you remember the Insta-days before reels?) and I had absolutely no intention of sharing my own projects. However, working on my 'reno home' took me on the most uplifting, empowering and unexpected journey. Through my discovery of DIY, I learned practical skills that I never knew I had in me, and I began to share DIY tutorials and home decor ideas for house projects on social media under the handle @houseprojectuk. I often marvel how this came about, but I firmly believe that the DIY girlie/grafter is within all of us. We just need the tools, the techniques and the time, and it's now my mission to share all of these with you in this book so that no DIY task, big or small, feels intimidating, but rather a welcome challenge that promises immense satisfaction. (I'll refer to tools, techniques and time as 'The 3 Ts' in each project as we move through the chapters.)

Before we get cracking, I'd like to share a little more of my story, which started back in my childhood home in Birmingham, England. I lived there with my mom (if you're a true Brummie, you'll know that this is not a typo), my Dad and my two younger sisters. My parents lovingly maintained our three-bedroom terraced house and I have fond memories of Dad fixing everything. In fact, I can't ever recall seeing a tradesperson. Mom brought the creativity; with decor ideas I suspect were inspired by *Changing Rooms*, a BBC TV show that was popular in the late nineties and early noughties and featured home makeovers. Weekend trips to our local DIY store Do It All were frequent, and I remember hanging off the trolley as we scanned the aisles, breathing in the classic smells of oils, paint and sawdust. At home, we were always rearranging

the furniture, and my constant search for ways to make my little box room feel more 'me', such as decorating it with posters of my idols Paul McGrath and Paul Nicholls, always filled me with absolute joy. (If you are too young to know who these people are, McGrath is an Aston Villa FC legend and Nicholls was a floppy-haired TV hottie.) Home was everything and I was very fortunate to have a wholesome childhood, filled with love and a lot of laughs.

Fast forward to 2006 and, as a Newly Qualified Teacher in Physical Education, I was firmly in the rental market. When you're moving every six to twelve months from mouldy flats to grotty shared houses, it can be hard to make a place feel like home. I tried though, and my penchant for cushions, photo frames and novelty fairy lights (it was the noughties) helped to make these spaces feel a little more 'mine'. However, damp walls, mouldy sealant and a lack of storage started to get my goat. I'd ask my landlords for a fresh coat of paint or to fix a broken blind, but they were largely disinterested, and the lettings agent reminded me that in the contract it stated 'rented as seen'.

Flying ahead to 2012, I met a man. *Finally!* Still teaching PE, I met a fellow PE teacher who became the Ant to my Dec. Basically, my better half. He was a whizz in the kitchen and loved to manage the food shopping, meal prep and basically all culinary exploits. He was doing what my Mom had always done at home. But as our relationship progressed to marriage, then two children in 19 months (jeez!), and our careers developed and we moved from a 17th-century terraced house to a mastic-fresh new-build home, I realized that there were lots of things that were not being done. The blackout blind in the kids' room remained in the box and the feature wall I craved in the bedroom remained, well, featureless. It was 2015, and it was very much the 'feature wall era'! I sound terrible here, but as much as I liked being cooked for, I also really wanted blinds to be put up and jobs to be done around the house! Slowly, it dawned on me that my experience of who fulfilled the roles at home was perhaps a little dated.

WHY WAS I NOT JUST DOING IT?
In 2019, with a one- and three-year-old, my husband and I bought a renovation project, inspired solely by all the property programmes that were broadcast every night on TV. We spontaneously bought a house after driving past and seeing the For Sale sign. It needed work but was bigger, had more garden and was in a nicer area. Deal done, and four months later we moved in. I was now a SAHM (stay-at-home mother), pausing my 13-year career somewhat reluctantly, but doing what needed to be done for the family. My days were spent drinking tepid coffees at playgroups and trying to avoid the hazards that our pre-reno home offered to the little ones. To be completely honest, I found this transition hard. I had gone from being a leader in my school role to feeling fairly invisible. And I spent many, many hours in a home that needed EVERYTHING doing to it. I then badly injured my knee, rupturing my ACL (anterior cruciate ligament) while having my weekly adult escape, sorry, runaround, with my local netball team, and soon after the 2020 Covid lockdown arrived. Now even more confined to my home, wearing a full leg-brace and experiencing increasing resentment towards the burgundy deep-pile carpet and Artex, I felt lost, without any sense of freedom or satisfaction or inner sparkle.

However, this is the time when things started to turn around. This is an empowering and positive book, I promise, so stick with me. One day, during nap time, I decided to 'just do it'. The 'it' was a peg rail that we'd bought for my daughter's room. I wanted to put it up, but I 'didn't do' drilling, or rather I'd never used a drill. But I did have a memory of watching my Dad wield one, and also my husband, somewhat reluctantly. Therefore, I measured the holes, I marked the wall and then drilled a slightly messy hole. I then drilled a second hole, which was a little bit better, and popped a plug inside each one. I say 'popped' because the holes were too big and I pushed in the plugs with my fingers! I screwed the peg rail into the wall using the only screwdriver I could find, and I realized I had just kind of done it! The rail held, and it was great to see it off the floor and on the wall. It wasn't perfect, but it wasn't a disaster!

As time progressed and I started to look for guidance and inspiration online, my interest in watching other people's DIY projects grew into an obsession. I decided to try panelling and some upcycling. I started to film the makeovers and share them on my own Instagram account. Slowly but surely, my confidence grew. I was absolutely winging it, but I think showing my mistakes and being honest about them was quite helpful to others. Before long, I had taught myself a whole range of new skills through discovery, trial and error, and perseverance. At the age of 36, I had found something that I really looked forward to doing and that I could do in my own space and at my own pace, which was exactly what I needed. I was making progress in the house, which made me feel happier, and the satisfaction and pride that came with mastering a project gave me my biggest sense of achievement. To be completely honest, my ego also thrived off the feedback I received from followers. Thumbs-up emojis and hearts on my social media posts felt like the smiles and occasional nods of approval I used to get from the students I taught, and spurred me on to try more. Being a SAHM was such an emotionally rich experience, but I was grateful I had also carved out something I could do for myself. Now don't get me wrong, not everything has been plain sailing and there have been countless bodged jobs along the way, resulting in a mad panic trying to put them right before my husband returns from work. But through these mistakes I have learned to fill, caulk and repair too!

In 2021, I returned to teaching part-time, but me and my weak knee moved across to the science department. The children went to school and nursery, and I continued to work on my home and share it on Instagram. Juggling projects, teaching and family life has been a challenge I have relished. We started the major part of our home renovation and I learned to upholster, panel, build and decorate. I have since been fortunate enough to speak at Grand Designs Live and receive an award for my DIY at the ufurnish.com Home Awards. And now, being offered the chance to write this book has been the greatest challenge and accolade of my life. The teacher in me wants to educate, and the content creator wants to inspire and motivate, so I hope to achieve a combination of all three by sharing these house projects with you. I also want to normalize the learning process within our homes.
Where else would we ever attempt a new skill and expect perfection first time? So let's normalize the mistakes and those 'Oh sh*t!' moments. It is going to happen. It is part of the journey, but the learning curve is steep and you probably won't make the same mistake again.

I dedicate this book to my family, who have supported me relentlessly, and to my online followers, who have encouraged me and been my greatest cheerleaders.
And I still marvel that all of this came out of an impatient decision one day to pick up a drill and give it a go. This is the book I wish I had by my side when I first attempted to DIY. You've got this! Your DIY journey starts here.

Laura

The first of our '3 Ts' are TOOLS. The key to getting started is knowing what you need for the task and where you can get it from. Large DIY stores can be overwhelming with their endless aisles and jargon-laden signage, so I like to simplify and especially differentiate between what is essential and what is desirable. I often look at my tools in the same way that I view my wardrobe. The majority of my 'capsule collection' of clothes is made up of staple items (in my case, jeans and black tops) but there are also a few sequins that get worn once a year! Similarly, with tools, there are the must-have pieces that are complete utility items, with many versatile functions that are totally worth investing in, versus the 'once in a while' tools that are not going to get used as much. A few of these can be good to own, but others are not worth the expense and are much better to hire for specific jobs.

Each project in this book will feature a Toolbox so you can identify which tools are needed for each project. Access to tools is a major barrier to getting started, but borrowing off family or co-owning between friends is a great way of pooling resources. A while ago, I started asking for 'tool money' contributions as a present idea for Christmas and birthdays. Glamorous? Not really. But it fuelled my hobby, and my family love contributing to something that is actually useful, plus the joy of unwrapping a cordless multi-tool with its universal battery and handy storage bag is unrivalled! Seriously, don't knock it until you try it.

So here is what is in my toolbox and why…

TOOL CLUB

THE BASICS

Let's start with the basics. These fundamental items need to be in every toolbox and are the cheapest items you can buy. They do not require charging and are great starter items with which you can attempt most of the house projects in this book.

NO POWER TOOLS AND BUDGET FRIENDLY

SAFETY GLASSES/DUST MASK ❶
Your safety is the most important thing. Cutting materials, sanding and even painting can lead to dust particles and fumes. Protect your eyes from these hazards (even in the quick 'oh just do it now' DIY moments). A dust mask will also reduce the inhalation of potentially harmful dust particulates.

TAPE MEASURE ❷
These are available in every shape, size and colour, but investing in a good-quality 5-metre metal retractable tape measure is essential. Tape measures are labelled as Class 1 or Class 2, which indicates their accuracy. Most widely available tape measures are Class 2, which will be adequate for your day-to-day measuring jobs. However, if you are doing more specialist work, such as carpentry, I recommend investing in a Class 1 type. And remember the old proverb, measure twice and cut once!

CLAW HAMMER ❸
The V-shaped claw is essential for gently removing nails from walls and timber. In the long term, for a comprehensive toolbox, you may wish to invest in a rubber mallet and a lump hammer. However, they are not required for any of the DIY jobs in this book.

SCREWDRIVER SET ❹
Do you know your Phillips from your flat-head? They are both manual screwdrivers that allow you to insert and remove screws. However, the Phillips has a cross-shaped tip, designed to fit and turn screws with corresponding cross-shaped slots on the head. This design helps to centre the screwdriver on the screw and reduces the risk of slipping. In contrast, a flat-head screwdriver has a wedge tip, which fits screws that have a single notch in the screw head. Investing in a multiset of manual screwdrivers will allow you to tighten and finish many of the DIY projects featured in this book.

WALL PLUG AND SCREWS ASSORTMENT ❺
Wall plugs and rawl plugs are the same thing. Initially named after the brand founder Joseph Rawlings, they are plugs that are used to anchor screws into walls. We will cover the 'how' in Build It (see page 64), but for the best value, invest in a multipack of screws with corresponding wall plugs.

PANEL SAW ❻
A hand saw or panel saw is used for making straight cuts and is a great starter tool to add to your collection. The TPI rating indicates the number of 'teeth per inch' and the higher the number, the finer the finish. A low TPI is ideal for a fast cut, but the finish will be coarser. The Build It chapter (see page 64) explores cutting materials.

MITRE BOX ❼
To make cuts that join, knowing your angles is very important. A mitre box shows you the angles and enables you to guide the saw smoothly through your cutting material. The most basic mitre box will feature cutting guides at 45 and 90 degrees.

SPIRIT LEVEL ❽
A humble spirit level is a must-have item for your toolbox, essential for DIY but also for those fun decorative jobs. Just pop it against your surface and the spirit bubble will tell you if you are level (horizontal measurements) or plumb (perpendicular measurements). They are less accurate than a laser level, which can give you a level line around your room, so if you're installing panelling, a dado rail or aligning your gallery wall, then a laser level would be a good investment.

CLAMPS ❾
Plastic or metal, clamps are great for when you need an extra pair of hands. They are especially good for securing cutting materials and holding items while they dry on both sides. A multipack of clamps in different sizes is highly recommended.

CARTRIDGE GUN ❿
This is also referred to as a caulking or sealant gun and is essential for a smooth application of filler, adhesive, sealant or decorator's caulk. Prices vary massively but, for the occasional job, a cheaper one will do the trick. If you want a little more help with the trigger, electric ones will keep it moving smoothly. Check page 31 for caulking tips.

STUD FINDER/WALL SCANNER ⓫
To know what lies behind your walls, a stud finder is an essential tool to locate the position of the wooden studs that sit behind your plasterboard. Locating these allows for a more secure fixing and reduces the damage to your plasterboard. A wall scanner will detect the location of electrical wiring and metal pipes, which are essential to locate before drilling into a wall.

DECORATING TOOLS ⓬
Painter's tape
Masking tape
Protective sheets
Scraper tool
Filling knife
Paintbrushes and rollers (see more on page 124)
Paint scuttle
Roller tray

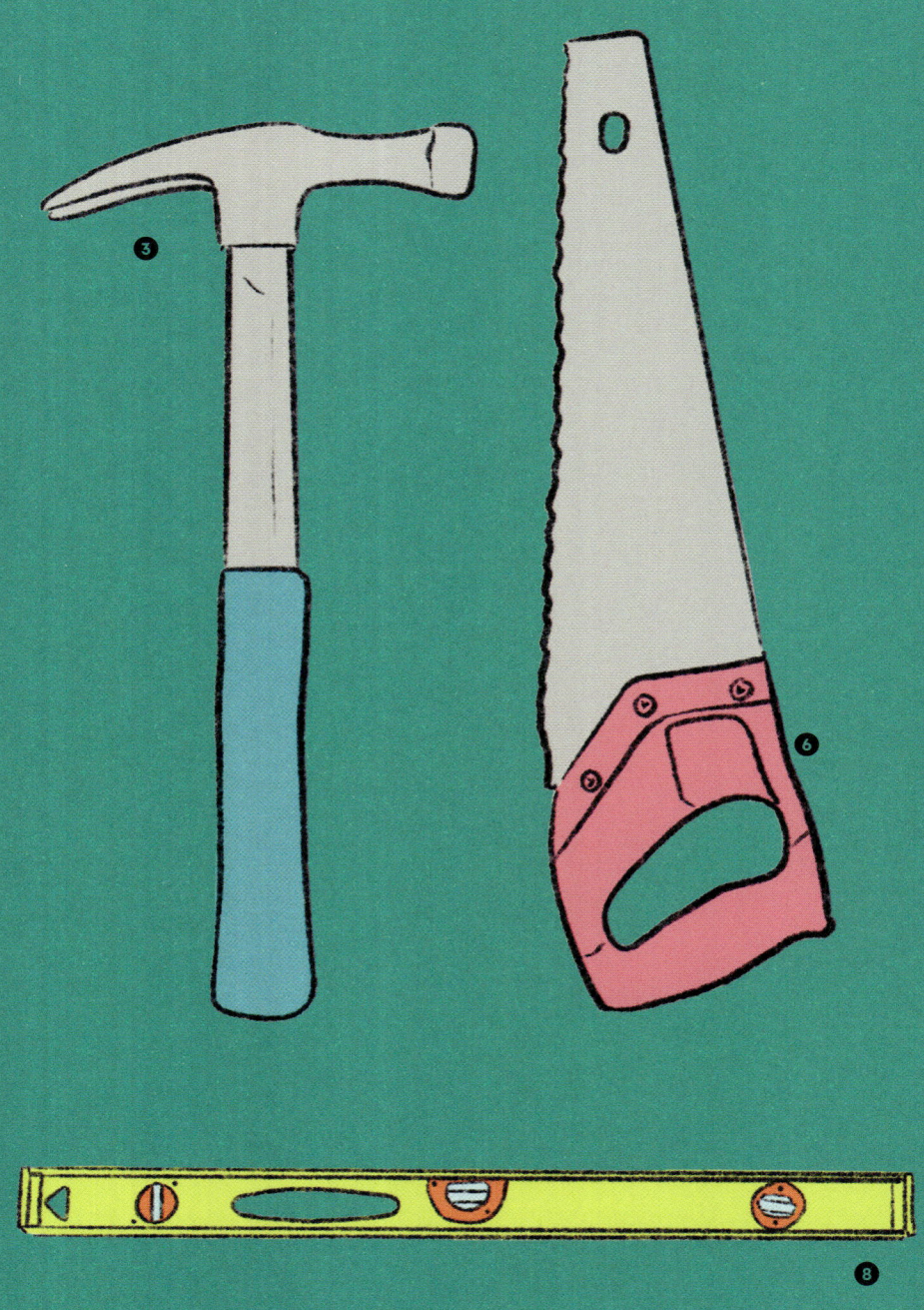

TOOL CLUB

THE POWER

If you are looking to build a power-tool collection, here are the key items to buy. Investing in an established brand, which has the capacity to share charging batteries, is also recommended as it spares you the need for multiple separate charging docks. I also don't know anyone who has regretted buying a cordless power tool! Safety eyewear is a must when using any of these tools.

THE TOOLS THAT WILL TAKE YOUR PROJECTS TO THE NEXT LEVEL

COMBI DRILL ❶
When I polled my followers, 'the drill' was the most feared power tool. However, if you want to secure fixings in your home, it is also one of the most important. A combi drill is a very versatile tool and essential for many DIY jobs as it can drill into a variety of materials and the hammer action makes it suitable for brick and masonry too. However, if you require more 'oomph' for drilling tougher materials, a hammer drill makes light work of those heavy-duty jobs.

ELECTRIC SCREWDRIVER ❷
This truly is your DIY buddy. An electric screwdriver can turn a flat-pack into something spectacular in no time at all, plus it's also necessary for tightening screws around the home, and especially when hanging load-bearing items on walls (see pages 86–94). Their reverse function will also help with the easy removal of screws from your walls or furniture.

JIGSAW ❸
A jigsaw allows you to create those freeform shapes and curves that are 'oh-so-trendy' right now and, with the correct blade, can cut through wood, steel and aluminium. A standard machine will come with a minimum of two blades, so check the TPI (teeth per inch) to get the right one for your job. A jigsaw can cause huge vibrations, so secure your material to a table or workbench with clamps to reduce the impact this has on you.

ELECTRIC SANDER ❹
An electric sander is far more efficient than manually using sandpaper and a block. See page 29 for the lowdown on 'grit' and different models to consider when making a purchase. My first sander was a corded 'mouse sander' that was small but powerful enough to take on my first upcycles and panelling projects. Protective eyewear and a dust mask are essential when sanding.

NAIL GUN/STAPLE GUN ❺
A nail gun will allow you to secure materials together with speed and precision and can really help with repetitive DIY jobs, such as securing skirting and panelling, or creating a firm fix between the fabric, wadding and wood in upholstery projects. Sometimes advertised as a 'finishing nail gun', prices can vary hugely, but a cordless battery-powered nail gun is often enough to give you a professional-looking result. See page 111 for a simple bench seat project, which is perfect for building your skills with a staple gun.

CIRCULAR SAW ❻
A circular saw is ideal for cutting large sheets of materials for your projects, such as MDF panelling strips (see page 176), hardwood ply pegboard (see page 101) or DIY picture ledge (see page 98). Use it for straight cuts or adjust the blade for accurate bevel (angled) cuts. The rotating blade can be scary for DIY beginners, but if you buy a large sheet from a DIY store, many will have an in-store cutting team that can trim your material for you.

MULTI-TOOL ❼
A multi-tool is the Swiss army knife of the DIY world. It can cut, sand and scrape, and its additional heads mean it can get into the tight corners that larger power tools can't access. For small DIY projects, investing in one of these may mean you need fewer individual power tools, depending on the size of your DIY projects.

TOOL CLUB

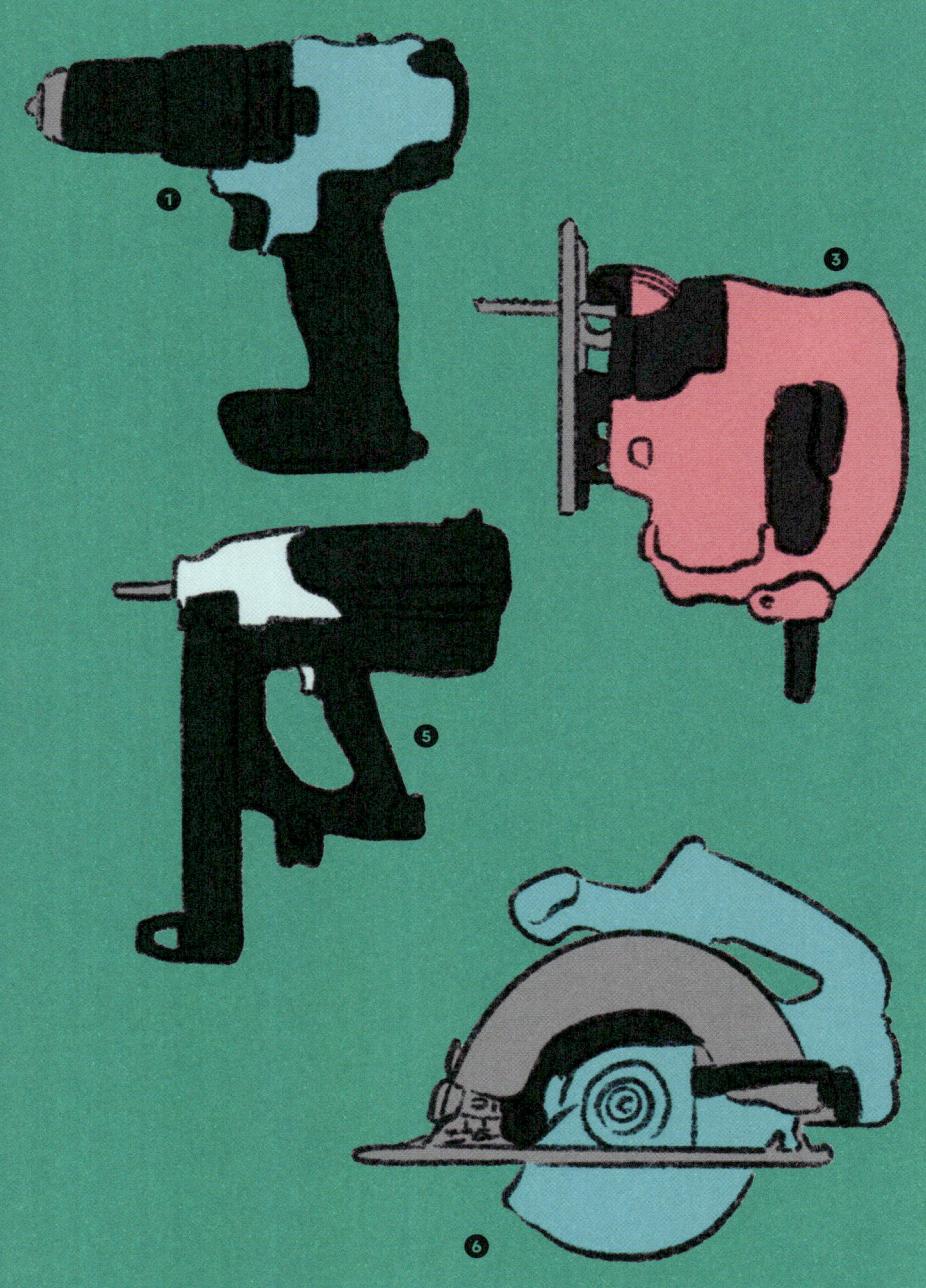

TOOL CLUB

TIME

LET'S FACE IT, WE CAN WANT TO TAKE ON DIY TASKS, BUT TIME RESTRICTIONS AND CONCERN ABOUT THE CHALLENGES INVOLVED OFTEN MEAN THEY SLIP DOWN THE 'TO-DO LIST'.

The second part of 'The 3 Ts' is TIME. Fitting house projects around the many demands life places on us can be difficult. Therefore, in this book, each project has been issued a time rating so you can quickly assess if it is doable for you in the time you have available. Some projects are super quiet, so perfect for times when little children are sleeping, or for a late-night sesh that won't upset the neighbours! Other projects need your full commitment, so require time blocking in the calendar for you to have the chance to give them your full focus.

Thankfully, many projects in this book are ones that can be picked up and put back down, without leaving too much mess behind. They allow you to complete phase one and then close the door until you have time to reconvene. When looking at project timings, it is important to remember that DIY is just like a hobby, a recreational activity you do for pleasure and get a sense of achievement from. As with any hobby, if you overdo it, you experience fatigue and frustration and then inevitably make mistakes. Which is also okay! But to maximize enjoyment and satisfaction, it is important to pick projects that are suited to your skill set!

You can also be more efficient by planning ahead. Think about the materials you will need for the job and order supplies online during the week leading up to a project, or buy them on the way home from work to help you avoid losing the first 2 hours of your 'DIY Do-Day' queuing in a busy DIY store on a Saturday morning.

QUICK & QUIET
is for all those jobs that can fit perfectly into your day without major disruption. Maybe during your lunch break, a child's nap time or you have a spare couple of hours. These house projects have a clearly defined start and end, require minimal tools and won't cause disruption that might upset the neighbours.

HALF DAY
for the jobs we start first thing and are finished by lunch. Often these are prep or snagging jobs that help get a room project across the line. Plan for 3—4 hours and factor in a tea break half-way through — with biscuits — as it's essential!

FULL DAY
is for the projects that require some preparation and may involve drying time. These projects are made up of multiple phases and can often take a full day to complete. If you do not have a full day to spare, break the project down into small, manageable parts to fit your schedule.

THE WEEKENDER
is when you have big goals and have blocked time out to tackle the project. To maximize your time, get your tools and materials ready the night before. If relevant, do any measuring up or colour-choosing ahead of time too so no time is wasted. Pop the kettle on and get ready to smash it!

SHE BELIEVED SHE COULD,

SO SHE WENT & BLOODY SMASHED IT.

One quote I recall clearly from my teacher-training days is that 'failing to prepare is preparing to fail'. Not only is this true in the world of education, but it is also fundamental in order to succeed with your DIY projects. Failing to prepare your teaching resources may affect a particular lesson, but failing to prep fresh plaster for paint may lead to the excruciating agony of seeing the gains from your hard-spent weekend literally peeling off in front of your eyes. Yes, the prep often takes time. It can be tedious, and who likes spending money on the boring stuff you don't really see! But believe me, it is so worth it.

In this chapter we will focus on the removing, filling, sanding, priming and treating of household materials. Having these basic skills in your locker will give you the confidence to try more advanced DIY projects, plus they also provide an insurance policy for when things don't quite go to plan as they help you to repair and renew, so you can start all over again! Learning to fill holes effectively is a great skill to master, and I like to think of it as like having an emergency parachute or a concealer for your eye bags. Being able to rescue projects and cover up mistakes (be they yours or the previous homeowners') is an essential skill for your repertoire.

Stripping and sanding effectively can also be incredibly rewarding, as these skills can help salvage period features, such as an original fireplace or wooden floorboards, or revive thrifted pieces of furniture, thereby preserving the history of your home or boosting the project budget by transforming furniture you already own. They are also a key stepping stone towards the decorative and aesthetic parts of home improvement!

So, grab your PPE, and let's deep dive into all things 'prep'.

PREP IT

SANDING

In many of the DIY projects outlined in this book, you will need to prepare your chosen material by sanding. Sanding sounds simple, right? But it is important to choose the correct grit and think about the type of sander you will use to get the best result for your project. A sanding block and sheet of sandpaper can work for some tasks, but a power sander offers speed and efficiency and is a great tool for your DIY journey.

Orbital sanders work by rapidly rotating the sanding disc, giving a smooth finish without noticeable edges. They cannot access corners or intricate detailing, but they are ideal for large, flat surfaces such as walls or furniture panels. For the corners you can't reach with an orbital, a detailed sander or palm sander has a flat edge that can get into smaller, or intricate corners. These are cheaper and a great starter tool to add to your collection. For larger renovation projects, like sanding floorboards, you can either hire or invest in a belt sander to strip back old paint and wood finishes.

PREP IT

PROTECT YOURSELF AND YOUR FURNITURE

```
PPE stands for 'personal protective equipment'
and is a must for the keen, or even reluctant, DIYer.
This starts with wearing clothing that is tough and
hardwearing to protect the skin. Safety glasses will
protect your eyes from dust, debris and fumes that
can irritate or cause injury. Dust extraction is so
important to reduce the possible inhalation of
dangerous particles. Sanders that connect to your
vacuum cleaner are recommended, and a dust mask is a
must for any sanding projects. Invest in dust sheets
to protect your furniture and surroundings. You can
spend more on reusable, cotton dust sheets that can
be stored away in between your DIY jobs, or try
plastic decorating sheets with optional masking tape
attached. It is so important to invest in these
pieces of protective equipment to safely approach
all of your future projects.
```

TOP TIPS FOR SUCCESS
- Always sand with the grain, which means moving your sandpaper in the same direction as the wood grain.
- Start with a low-grit and move up to the finer-grit papers.
- Clean the dust off the material and sanding disc in between grits.
- You can add a light pencil mark to the material and change grit once the pencil mark has been removed.

A GUIDE TO GRIT
Knowing your 'grit' is key to making your project a success. Every piece of sandpaper is graded and this number corresponds to the size of the abrasive particles on the paper, which determines how coarse or fine the paper is. There are specialist types that sit at the extreme ends of the scale, but the papers most commonly used in DIY are…

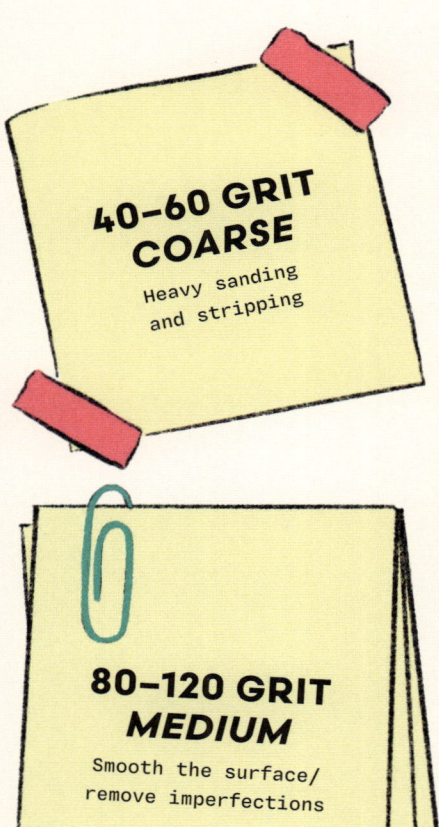

40–60 GRIT
COARSE
Heavy sanding and stripping

80–120 GRIT
MEDIUM
Smooth the surface/ remove imperfections

150–180 GRIT
FINE
Final phase before the wood is painted/stained

220–224 GRIT
VERY FINE
Use in between coats of primer or paint to smooth brush marks or minor imperfections

PREP IT

FILLING

Filler is an essential part of your decorating kit, as it can be used to repair cracks, holes and small gaps in many different home surfaces, such as plaster, wood and masonry. Purchase it ready-mixed in tubs or cartridges for speedy applying and drying, with no need for messy mixing. You will need filling knives to spread the filler and a fine-grit sandpaper to get a smooth finish once the filler has dried. Choose a specific filler for your task as the properties of each product will help you achieve the optimum finish. A flexible filler will dry hard and bind a gap, but will contract and expand with changes in temperature. This is ideal for filling cracks in plaster so that they do not reappear. Wood fillers are tinted to blend in with the wood finish, whereas plaster fillers dry with a smooth and often white powdered finish that can then be sanded and painted to blend with the existing wall. We will cover these more specifically on pages 44–52, so that you can achieve the perfect finish, whatever your DIY task.

THE ART OF CAULKING

Caulk is a waterproof seal that can be applied to fill gaps up to 6mm. Most caulks are paintable and can conceal joins and seal edges, which can then be covered with paint for a professional-looking finish. Caulking the join between your wall and skirting board, or along the top of a dado rail will give your project a professional finish. You may have heard the saying 'try your best and caulk the rest!' — the perfect mantra for the beginner, which also means that learning how to caulk represents a milestone in the rite of passage of every novice DIYer. Think of it as the make-up concealer of the DIY world: used correctly, it can help give a flawless result; used badly, it draws attention to that area you want to hide! However, there are simple ways to ensure your caulk application goes from blobby to beautiful. In our panelling chapter (see page 164), caulk is used prior to priming and painting to create a seamless finish between the timber and the wall.

WHAT YOU NEED
You just need a tube of 'decorator's caulk', which is budget-friendly and available in all DIY stores, and a caulking gun. Before placing the tube in the gun, you will need to snip the nozzle to create a small hole. Cut it at an angle and towards the tip of the nozzle so the hole is small. If you cut it too large, too much product will come out and the flow of caulk will be difficult to control. If in doubt, start about 6mm from the nozzle tip.

HOW TO CAULK
Normally I am a 'YOLO/what's the worst that can happen' kind of girl, but I really do suggest you practise your caulking technique. Take a scrap of wood or an offcut of cardboard packaging and have a practice at running a bead of caulk along the edge. The important thing is to keep the caulk gun moving. If you go too slowly, the product will build up and you will get lumps and bumps. If you go too fast, the product can stretch, and your thin line will not cover the required area. Hold it steady and move smoothly. You'll instantly know when you are in your groove, and it is oh-so satisfying!

HOW TO CREATE A SMOOTH FINISH

After applying caulk it's important to smooth the finish, and there are three options to choose from (see below). Your caulk will stay wet enough to smooth for about 5 minutes, so if you are inexperienced, apply a bead of caulk and smooth it straight after, before applying another bead elsewhere. Then, once the caulk has thoroughly dried (I advise you leave it for 24 hours) you will be able to paint over it using wall emulsion paint or any wood finishes of your choice.

A **A wet finger** – run your finger along the surface of the caulk and wipe off the excess with a wet cloth.

B **A damp sponge** – rinse the sponge frequently to ensure the excess does not transfer back onto the wall.

C **A sealant kit** – available online and from DIY stores, these small silicone tools come in different shapes and sizes so you can find the edge that is perfect for your project. Run the tool along the caulk line with smooth, even pressure and keep removing the excess caulk.

CAULKING A BATHROOM

If you need to seal around a shower/bathroom fixture, you will need to use a silicone product instead (see page 60). Due to the high temperatures and moisture in a bathroom, the seal needs to be elastic and flexible. Silicone is formulated to be highly water resistant and durable – the bead will not shrink after application, which is ideal for forming a tight seal in damp areas. Best of all, it is available in different colours so you can match it to your existing grout or choose a clear sealant to achieve a sleek and contemporary join.

PS. You cannot paint silicone! I tried once – it doesn't work! (I told you this was the book I needed when I was starting out!)

HOW TO FILL WOOD

If you want to replace door handles, repair a piece of scratched wooden furniture or salvage existing floorboards, knowing how to fill wood successfully will allow you to reduce imperfections and create a smooth finish. This can then be painted or treated to your desired look. However, there is no 'one size fits all' formula here, and the product and technique you need will vary depending on the scale of the cavity you wish to fill.

WOOD FILLER
For a medium-sized hole (for example, you have removed door hardware) you will want to 'pack' the hole with wood. This will make the hole drillable again and also give a smooth finish. Use a piece of wooden dowel that is as close to the hole diameter as possible. Score the edges of the dowel gently, then cover it in wood glue and insert into the hole. You may need to hammer the dowel into the hole to achieve a snug fit. If the dowel protrudes, it can be sanded back to achieve a smooth finish.

EPOXY RESIN
Alternatively, larger holes can be filled with an epoxy-resin product, which creates a tough and durable bond and is ideal for larger projects like floorboard restoration or for larger cavities in wooden furniture. Epoxy resin comes in two parts: the epoxy acts like a glue to bind and fill the gap, while the resin hardens and cures. Before the resin is fully dry, you can even add the texture of wood by carving into the surface to help blend it with the existing wood. This is definitely more cost-effective than replacing floorboards, but when epoxy resin is used in large quantities it can take up to 72 hours to harden, which can impact the use of a room! Make sure to read the manufacturer's instructions to get the best results.

STRIPPING

To get the best finish on something that has previously been painted or varnished, we need to strip it right back. Removing layers of old paint can feel like uncovering a time capsule as you get to see all of the piece's previous colours and finishes through the years. That means using manual work or chemicals to remove the layers of existing topcoat. Depending on the age or condition of your wood, this may be a quickish job or a total labour-intensive nightmare.

HOW TO STRIP PAINT OR VARNISH

There are three main methods of removing paint or varnish from woodwork, and your choice will be determined by where it is in your home, the size of the project and how much available time you have. One thing is for sure, stripping off old paint is satisfying and excruciating in equal measure. However, it can also be smelly, so ensure you are working in a well-ventilated space and, if you can, keep kids and animals well away from this DIY! We'll discuss the safety concerns in more detail as we move through these projects, but ensure you have your dust mask and safety glasses ready.

If you are renovating an old house, you will encounter different hazards to if you are DIYing a more modern home. One of these hazards is the presence of lead paint. Lead was traditionally added to paint to speed up the drying process and to add durability to the finish. In 1992 lead paint was banned in the UK due to its toxicity, but it was banned much earlier in 1978 in the USA. It is important to test old paint for lead, as removing lead paint can be extremely hazardous. Lead test swab kits are readily available from DIY stores and online, and they will give you a result in less than a minute so that you know that you are safe to strip! If you do have lead paint, you have two choices: you can either paint over it or remove it. Purchasing 'encapsulation' specialist paint can be applied over the surface of lead paint to seal it. However, if the lead paint surface is flaking or in poor condition then it needs to be removed. Depending on the scale of the job, you can call in professionals to take care of the job for you or remove it yourself. DEFRA advise the use of chemical or caustic stripper instead of sanding to reduce dust or fumes. Wear protective clothing, gloves, a face mask with filter conforming to EN143 P2, and shut off the area you are working in to prevent the dispersal of particles to other areas of your home. Follow the instructions of your specific paint stripper, but once the majority of paint is off, use a dampened piece of sandpaper to remove the final traces. Moistened sandpaper will reduce the dispersal of those toxic particles. So, work slowly and take care.

Cover furniture and carpets completely and if the work continues into a second day, store your clothing in a sealed bag and ensure you wash your hands and skin thoroughly.

SANDING
A sheet of sanding paper wrapped around a sanding block can be used to remove smaller areas of paint by hand. This can be a cost-effective way to rub back a smooth surface and also to work the paper into curves and details in architraves or on skirting boards. However, if you are working on a large area, such as refurbishing floorboards, then hiring a sander can be an effective way of removing layers of paint or varnish. Be sure to work with the grain of the wood and start with a low-grit sandpaper, before working gradually up to a fine finish. See page 28 for everything you need to know about sanding.

HEAT GUN
A heat gun can be very effective at removing paint from wood, but does not work so well with varnish. It works by directing hot air through a nozzle, which causes old layers of paint to bubble. You can then go in with a scraper and lift the paint clean off the wooden surface. Every heat gun comes with a variety of different nozzles, and it is crucial that the right one is used for the right job. For example, if you are working in close proximity to glass, such as stripping a window or door frame, you must use the 'protection nozzle' with a narrow end that allows you to direct the heat onto a very precise zone. However, for large jobs away from glass, such as staircases or skirting boards, use the wide 'surface nozzle' that allows for a broader flow of hot air.

CHEMICAL STRIPPER

There are many chemical strippers on the market and their main advantage is that they can be applied into the nooks and crannies of intricately carved wooden features. Chemical strippers are categorized as 'solvent' or 'caustic' and consist of harsh chemicals to which exposure to the skin, or inhalation, can be very dangerous to your health. These should be used sparingly and in a well-ventilated area. Solvent strippers contain acetone, methanol, toluene and mineral spirit which have replaced methylene chloride, which was banned in the UK in 2012 due to its carcinogenic properties. Be wary if you find an old tin of paint stripper at the back of the shed as this might not adhere to modern safety standards. A caustic solvent contains sodium hydroxide which is alkaline and can break down the paint due to its high pH. Again this can cause skin burns, so be sure to follow all the advised safety precautions.

Solvent strippers are gentler than caustic ones, with no discolouration, so they are generally more suitable for use on antique furniture or intricate mouldings. They work well on ceiling beams, but are not so effective at removing heavy paint layers. You also often need to use a lot of product, which has a strong odour. In contrast, caustic strippers can remove thick layers of paint (of most finishes) and are especially good for stripping pine doors. They enable you to work fast and produce fewer fumes than solvents, but they can stain hardwoods and turn them black. So those pine doors would need to be repainted after they have been stripped.

If the use of chemicals in your home does not sound like a job you wish to take on yourself, then search online for a local company to do the job for you.

- Wear your PPE when doing a patch test. This is your first experience with the product too!

- Apply the product using a natural or plastic bristle brush to the thickness recommended by the product manufacturer.

- Leave it to do its thing — each product will have a specific work time ranging from a few minutes to 24 hours!

- The paint may bubble, blister or just soften during this time.

- Remove using a putty knife, gently pushing the softened paint back to reveal what lies beneath.

- Clean up using a soft cloth — white spirit can be used to remove sticky residue.

Based on the effectiveness of your patch test, you can decide if the product is right for you and if the 'working time' was sufficient to lift the paint.

HOW TO USE CHEMICAL STRIPPERS

Before using on a wider area, do a patch test wearing PPE as recommended opposite. Allow 48 hours prior to starting your project to assess how effective the patch test has been. As previously mentioned, caustic strippers can cause scorching and staining, so testing on a small discreet area is advised. For example, an area of floorboard in a corner, the back of a piece of furniture or the underside of a banister.

HOW TO USE A HEAT GUN

A heat gun 'does what it says on the tin', so to speak, and the intense heat does mean that there are risks involved, so ensure you follow these guidelines:

- Wear thick gloves and a mask to avoid burns and any inhalation of paint particles.

- Ensure the heat gun does not come into contact with flammable substances or surfaces. If you are working on your stair spindles, be sure to keep it away from the carpet or any pressurized containers.

- Keep the heat gun moving to avoid scorching. Never hold it statically over the wood. If there is a stubborn patch, leave that part and sand instead.

- Allow the nozzle of the heat gun to cool before placing it on the floor. The nozzle will remain hot for at least a minute after turning the gun off, so take care when handling it.

- Your smoke alarm is very likely to go off! You may wish, temporarily, to tape a plastic bag over it while you are using the heat gun to avoid it going off every 30 seconds. However, be sure to remove the bag as soon as you are finished!

WALLPAPER STRIPPING

Moving to a wallpapered home can be like walking into a time warp, where patterns and prints of yesteryear adorn the walls and stamp it firmly in an era. Or perhaps it is indeed your own previous wallpaper choices which have expired. Never fear, it can be removed to reveal a new fresh blank canvas, or more likely an exposed wall that now needs a bit of restoration! We'll cover wall prep once we have discussed wallpaper removal. There are several methods to remove wallpaper, and the decision will most likely be based on the condition of the existing wallpaper and wall, budget, and how much available time you have. Removal methods include steam or chemical strippers, or you can make a natural spray of white vinegar and water if you prefer to try a more budget- and environmentally friendly option. We'll take a closer look at these now.

But before we do, we once again need to make sure that personal safety is followed. Be sure to lay down protective sheets on flooring and over furniture, and wear safety glasses to protect your eyes. Whether you are using steam, chemical stripper or the natural vinegar method, keeping your eyes protected is important. If you're working at height, ensure you have a suitable ladder and that it is adequately supported.

REMOVING WALLPAPER BY HAND

When removing wallpaper by hand, you will need to score the wallpaper using a stripping tool/knife first to loosen the bond between the adhesive and the paper. Be careful not to score too hard so as not to mark the plaster. Whether you use steam or chemicals, these will need to soak into the paper and penetrate through the layers of adhesive. Hopefully your predecessors did not just wallpaper over old wallpaper, but often this process reveals a glimpse into the interiors of the past, which can be in equal parts exciting and time consuming.

REMOVING WALLPAPER WITH STEAM

For small projects, commercial wallpaper steamers are ideal. They're the kind of tool people only use once or twice, so ask around as there's a good chance someone you know has one sitting in their shed. For larger jobs, consider hiring a heavy-duty professional steamer for a small fee. The steamer works by heating up the water added to the tank and channelling this onto your wall through a steam plate. The moisture is absorbed into the paper, loosening the bond between the adhesive and the wall. This makes it easier to prise off with a scraper. See page 53 for step-by-step instructions on how to remove old wallpaper with steam.

REMOVING WALLPAPER WITH CHEMICAL STRIPPERS

If using chemical strippers, ensure you protect your skin from exposure by covering up and wearing your safety glasses and a mask to prevent inhalation of the fumes. Some chemical strippers are ready to apply, others can be purchased as a concentrated formula that requires dilution. Chemical strippers work by loosening the adhesion between the paper and the wall. They are good at working on stubborn areas of wall and work out cheaper than using a steamer. However, they require more manual application and introduce chemicals into the home. Look out for strippers that are VOC free.

Chemical strippers are simple to use. Using a wallpaper scorer, gently press into the paper to create small cuts or perforations, then liberally spray the area with stripper and leave to soak into the paper. Use a wallpaper stripping knife to gently push and scrape the paper off. Keep the knife at a flat angle as you scrape small sections of wallpaper away from the wall. Repeat the process on any stubborn sections of wallpaper adhesive residue.

DEALING WITH RUST

Rust marks can appear on anywhere from bathroom tiles, radiators, an outside patio or on metal furnishings. When unprotected metal is exposed to air and water, the surface can oxidize, leaving unsightly marks or staining contact surfaces. But all is not lost — these hacks will get your surface rust-free with just a little elbow grease. Be sure to grab those safety glasses again and wear a face mask to prevent the inhalation of nasty particles.

METAL
To remove rust from metal, lubricants like WD-40 can be sprayed onto the surface. Leave for 10 minutes, then use wire wool and gently rub away the surface rust.

RADIATORS
To remove rust spots from chrome radiators, take some aluminium foil and scrunch it into a tight ball, then rub it over the surface until the rust is removed.

INTERIOR TILES
To remove rust from interior tiles, all you need is a little lemon juice and white vinegar. This naturally acidic solution, mixed 1 part lemon juice to 1 part white vinegar, can be sprayed onto the rust to loosen the bond. Leave for 10 minutes, then scrub away the rust using an abrasive cloth.

EXTERIOR TILES
Garden furniture can often leave rust stains on patio tiles. For a spot clean, try the lemon juice and white vinegar solution above and leave for 30 minutes before scrubbing. However, if this is not sufficient to penetrate the stain, an abrasive cleaning product like The Pink Stuff can be applied using a cloth. Rub in a circular motion and rinse off with warm water.

It's time to bring the Pinterest board to life. These projects have been put together in the same way that you might find in a cookery book! What do you need? How long might it take? What comes first?

Kicking off with the essential prep projects, these will help you achieve the best finished result. Master these skills and you'll have the armoury to cope with any DIY disaster, as even the most accomplished DIYer will have to occasionally rectify a mistake. Once you've smashed the project prep, you'll move onto the intricacies of decorating. Knowing your tools and finishes will help you create and execute the interiors of your dreams! Then onto the finishing touches. Fancy trying a no-sew upholstery technique, designing the perfectly balanced gallery wall or looking to upcycle a thrifted piece? These projects will help bring your personal finish to your space and can be transferred into lots of different areas of your home. There are also projects that lean towards rental décor or for those looking for a budget-friendly update.

Panelling also needs its own moment. From panelling styles, their suitability for your room and how to measure up — you'll have it nailed in no time. Most importantly, they can all be modified to suit your home and style. If you need to scribble your measurements down, use the notes section (see pages 216–219) and make this a book you can work with to bring your ideas to life. Fold the corners, annotate and use these project guides to inspire and educate. You've got this!

The dimensions and measurements for these projects are in metric, however if you prefer to work with imperial measurements, please see page 216 for a conversion chart.

THE PROJECTS

HOW TO FILL A HOLE IN PLASTER

(DEPENDING ON THE SIZE OF THE HOLE)

If you've removed previous fixings (or maybe you've drilled in the wrong place), filling a hole is an essential skill to master.

TROUBLESHOOTING

If the plug does not come out of the wall, try this: Partway insert a new screw into the plug, then use the claw of your hammer to lever the screw gently and pull towards you to remove.

TOOLBOX
Dust protection sheet
Dust mask
Safety glasses
Dustpan and brush
Filling knife
Smooth finish/ fine finish plaster filler
High-grit sandpaper
Cloth
Mini roller
Paint

PREP IT

1. Remove any old wall plugs and screws from the wall. Using a dustpan brush, clear the hole of debris and dust.

2. Using a filling knife, push a small amount of smooth plaster filler into the hole, adding enough so that there is a little excess around the edges of the hole, then smooth it down and leave to dry. It is easier to build up layers than remove excessive amounts.

3. Using a high-grit sandpaper, sand down the excess filler until the wall is smooth. Clean the wall to remove any dust residue with a dustpan brush. A lightly dampened cloth will also remove dust, but be sure to let the area fully dry before moving on to step 4.

4. Using a mini emulsion roller, paint over the area and leave to dry. Feather out the edges of the fresh paint to blend in with the existing paint. However, this may still catch the light or 'flash' against the old paint finish. Discolouration of the old paint may mean your freshly painted area looks brighter and noticeable. If the existing wall is in poor condition, consider repainting the entire wall for a smooth and consistent finish.

FILLING SCREW HOLES IN WOOD

Gently sand and remove any splinters around the hole. Small holes left by removing screws can be filled by inserting wood filler into the hole using a putty knife or the narrow nozzle tip if using a cartridge. Overfill the hole then leave to dry. Sand down the excess using a high-grit sandpaper until you have a smooth finish.

HOW TO FILL A CRACK IN PLASTER

QUICK & QUIET

(DEPENDING ON THE SIZE)

It is inevitable that you will encounter cracks in your plaster at some point. Hairline cracks are common in new buildings, especially in the plaster around door frames and window recesses, and can be caused by the plaster drying out and the new building settling. However, shrinkage, temperature fluctuations or the poor application of plaster can lead to cracks appearing in buildings of any age. The only time you need to be concerned is if the crack is wider than 25mm as this can be an indicator of a structural problem. In every other case, you can simply fill the crack with a little simple DIY know-how.

TROUBLESHOOTING
Make sure you use a fine high-grit sandpaper for this job (see page 29) as anything coarse will leave indentations in the filler.

TOOLBOX
Dust protection sheet
Dust mask
Safety glasses
Stanley knife
Cartridge or caulking gun
Flexible filler
Microfibre cloth
Filling knife
Fine plaster filler
High-grit sandpaper
Dustpan and brush
Mini emulsion roller
Paint

PREP IT

1. Using a Stanley knife, cut into the crack, making it deeper and wider. This may seem counterintuitive, but you need to make it worse before it can get better. If you just patch the original crack with filler, it will be back within days. So, be brave!

2. Ensure there is no loose debris in the crack. The quickest way to do this is to run the small nozzle of the vacuum over the area.

3. Using a caulking gun, fill the enlarged crack with flexible filler. Cutting a 45-degree angle at the nozzle will allow you to directly apply it into the crack with precision, as the slanted cut directs the flexible filler and means that the hole, and therefore the bead applied, is not too big.

4. Using a damp microfibre cloth, wipe down the surface of the crack to remove any excess filler, then leave to dry for at least 4 hours.

5. Using a filling knife, apply fine plaster filler over the top of the flexible filler, then leave to dry for at least 2 hours. This final layer should be thin and allowed to dry before attempting the next step.

6. Using a high-grit sandpaper, sand back excess filler until you have a smooth, continuous wall surface. Brush off the dust residue using a dustpan brush and wipe clean using a damp cloth. Allow the wall to fully dry.

7. Using a mini emulsion roller, paint over the crack. Depending on the size of the crack and the wall, you may wish to completely repaint the wall to ensure there is no disparity in paint colour.

HOW TO CAULK A SKIRTING BOARD OR DOOR FRAME

QUICK & QUIET

To create a seamless join between wood and your wall, a bead of caulk is needed. We will refer to caulking the edge of your skirting board and door frame here, but the same technique is used for all caulking tasks referred to in this guide. Once executed correctly, it will finish off your panelling projects with professional poise, giving you a smooth and paintable finish.

TOOLBOX

Safety glasses
Dust protection sheets
Stanley knife
Caulk
Cartridge gun
Masking tape, if using
Damp sponge

TROUBLESHOOTING

- Remember to keep the caulk gun moving slowly. This will avoid the product stretching, or any lumps and bumps. Hold it steady and move smoothly.
- If this is your first time caulking and you are progressing slowly, apply a bead of caulk and smooth it straight after as you have about 5 minutes before it becomes too dry to smooth.

PREP IT

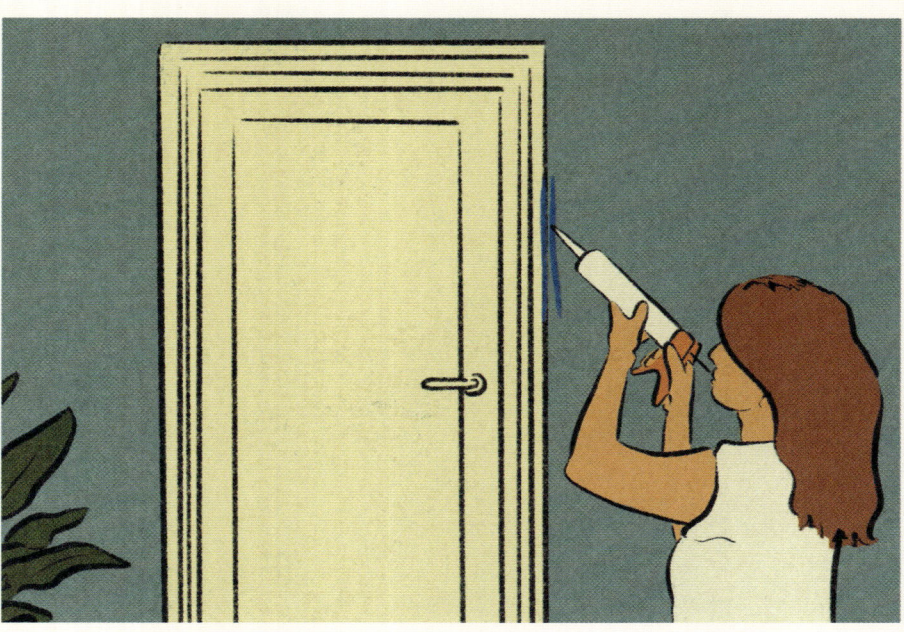

1. Remove any existing caulk carefully using a Stanley knife or a caulk removal tool. Clean the area thoroughly and allow it to dry. However, if you are adding new caulk to a project, do not worry about this and get ready for the next step.

2. Now for the snip! Cut the nozzle of the caulking tube at an angle and towards the tip of the nozzle to leave a small hole. If you cut it too large, too much product will come out and the flow of caulk will be difficult to control. If in doubt, start small (about 6mm from the nozzle tip).

3. Open the caulking gun by squeezing the release trigger at the back of the gun. While holding this trigger down, pull the long metal handle towards you — this will open up the caulking gun, allowing you to insert the cartridge into the base with the nozzle of the caulk now pointing away from you. Gently squeeze the trigger to apply pressure onto the caulking tube, keeping it secure.

4. It will take several pumps on the trigger to put enough pressure onto the base of the cartridge to release the caulk product. Test your technique on a spare piece of cardboard or timber before tackling the wall.

5. Use masking tape to mark the line you want to follow as this will keep the boundary neat.

6. Using the cartridge gun, apply the caulk and then smooth the finish with a wet finger, damp sponge or sealant tool (see page 32).

7. Once the caulk has thoroughly dried (it is advised to leave it 24 hours) you will be able to paint over it using wall emulsion or your choice of wood finish.

PREP IT

HOW TO FILL A LARGE HOLE IN WOOD

(DEPENDING ON THE SIZE OF THE HOLE)

TOOLBOX
Safety glasses
Wooden dowel
Utility knife
Wood glue
Sawdust
Medium- to high-
   grit sandpaper

If the hole is larger, wood filler is not a viable option, as it will crack. Wood filler is also unsuitable for exterior applications as wood shrinks and expands due to changes in temperature and moisture levels. There are a few different options to 'pack the hole' but let's outline two and you can decide what is best for your particular project and available time.

PACKING THE HOLE WITH WOOD

Packing the hole with wood will leave you with a smooth finish and will make the hole drillable again. The natural wood finish can also help match the colour finish.

PREP IT

1. Use a piece of dowel that is as close to the hole diameter as possible.

2. Score the edges of the dowel gently using a utility knife.

3. Cover the outside of the dowel with wood glue (optional extra: add saw dust into the wood glue to colour match).

4. Insert the dowel into the hole so that it is flush.

5. Lightly sand with medium-grit sandpaper before moving up to a higher fine-grit paper, in the direction of the grain.

6. Stain, varnish or paint to match the surrounding finish.

USING EXPOXY RESIN TO FILL A LARGE HOLE

Using epoxy resin to fill a large hole offers greater strength and durability than wood alone. The epoxy resin product comes in two parts. Follow the product manufacturer's guidance on timings.

TOOLBOX
```
Epoxy resin kit
Strong tape
High-grit
   sandpaper
```

1 Clean the hole out by rubbing the inside with sandpaper and remove any loose debris or dust with a brush or vacuum cleaner nozzle.

2 Tape one side of the hole with a strong tape to seal the hole and prevent leaks. Press down firmly and turn the wood back over so the hole is accessible.

3 Mix the epoxy and hardener to the ratio advised by the manufacturer.

4 Stir slowly to avoid trapping air bubbles in the thick liquid.

5 Pour slowly into the hole. The mixture will self-level as it settles into the hole.

6 Leave to cure (depending on size, this will need approximately 24 hours).

7 To finish, remove the tape and use a high-grit sandpaper to smooth any visible edges.

8 Stain, wax or paint to match the surrounding finish.

PREP IT

HOW TO REPAIR A CRACK IN A WOODEN FLOORBOARD

QUICK & QUIET

(DEPENDING ON THE SIZE)

If you have a crack in an old wooden floorboard, the application of ready-mixed wood filler or epoxy resin will do the trick (see page 51). However, you also have another option. If you have sawdust and wood glue, these can be combined to make a paste that works as a great filler and, if you have been sanding floorboards, you will have a perfect colour-matched product that, when mixed with wood glue, can seamlessly fill the crack.

TOOLBOX

```
Dust protection
  sheets
Dust mask
Safety glasses
Wood glue
Putty knife
High-grit
  sandpaper
Wood filler
Cartridge gun
Topcoat, if using
Fine paintbrush
Wood magic
  markers,
  if using
```

PREP IT

1. Clean the floor thoroughly with a vacuum cleaner followed by a damp mop to remove any dust, dirt or loose parts of the floorboard. Pay particular attention to the cracks and grooves in the floorboard.

2. Collect sawdust (the finer the better) — try to colour match by using sawdust from the same type of wood.

3. Combine the sawdust with wood glue in a container and mix to create a smooth, thick mixture.

4. Use a putty knife to apply the mixture into the crack. It may settle, so add more until the void is filled.

5. Leave to dry overnight.

6. Ensure the mixture has hardened and sand smooth with a high-grit sandpaper.

7. To finish, there are two ways you can blend the new area with the old:

   A Apply the same flooring topcoat over the crack using a small, thin brush. This may require two coats.

   B Purchase a set of wood magic markers that come in various shades of brown. The fine and thick nibs allow you to recreate the texture and markings of the floorboard. These are perfect for wood finishes that vary in tone.

HOW TO STEAM OFF OLD WALLPAPER

HALF DAY/ FULL DAY
(DEPENDING ON THE SCALE OF PROJECT)

Removing old wallpaper and replacing with new wallpaper can bring a dated space back to life. Using steam is a natural way of penetrating the paper and loosening the adhesive that sits behind and bonds it to the wall.

TOOLBOX
Dust protection sheets
Dust mask
Safety glasses
Ladder
Wallpaper scorer
Wallpaper steamer
Stripping knife

TROUBLESHOOTING
When allowing the steam to saturate the paper, be careful not to leave it for too long as the moisture can penetrate and damage the plaster behind.

1. Using a wallpaper scorer, gently press into the paper to create small cuts or perforations.

2. Add water to the steamer, ensure it is placed on an even surface, then turn it on and wait until the water is heated to the right temperature. (Adding warm water to the machine will speed up this process.)

3. Press the steamer head against the bottom corner of the wall and allow the steam to saturate the paper for about 10 seconds.

4. Move the steamer head to the next section of paper and pull up the previously steamed section. If it does not come away easily, use a stripping knife to gently scrape the paper away.

5. Keep moving the steamer head up the wallpaper drop until you have completely removed a section, then move along the wall and repeat, removing a section at a time.

PREP IT

HOW TO PREPARE WALLS FOR WALLPAPER

HALF DAY/ FULL DAY

(DEPENDING ON THE SCALE OF PROJECT)

In order to achieve the best results for your wallpaper project, it is important to prepare your walls first. Lumpy filler, holes or uneven paint textures will show through your paper, so it is worth taking the time to smooth and prep the surface.

TOOLBOX

Dust protection sheets
Dust mask
Safety glasses
Ladder
Fine-finish plaster filler
Medium-grit sandpaper
White emulsion paint or universal primer, if using
Lining paper, if using

TROUBLESHOOTING

Applying a light universal primer instead of emulsion paint is a little more expensive but can also provide a key for your wallpaper adhesive, which then helps grip the paper.

PREP IT

1. Remove any existing wall plugs or screws and fill the holes using a fine-finish plaster filler (see page 44).

2. If the wall has any visible bumps or texture, sand it down using a medium-grit sandpaper.

3. If the wall has been painted in a strong colour and you are opting for a light-coloured paper, you will need to roller a base coat of white emulsion onto the wall to avoid the strong colour showing through. If you do this, leave the paint to dry and cure for 48 hours before wallpapering.

4. To add lining paper or not to add lining paper? That is the question. It will depend on the condition of your walls. It does require extra labour, but it also prevents the wallpaper from shrinking when it dries and can stop those frustrating gaps between the drops of wallpaper. It also stops existing wall marks from showing through and is essential for areas that are exposed to damp as it provides a barrier and can improve the grip of your wallpaper.

HOW TO APPLY LINING PAPER

FULL DAY

Choosing a lining paper can feel as complicated as choosing a wallpaper. However, the main thing to know is that lining papers have different grades, so the lower the grade, the thinner the paper (and the higher the grade, the thicker the paper). It is widely recommended that a 1400 grade will be thick enough to cover imperfections, but still light enough to work with. Also, in my opinion, a 'paste-the-wall' lining paper is essential as this means you won't need a pasting table and can avoid a whole lot of mess. You won't regret it!

```
TOOLBOX
Dust protection
  sheets
Dust mask
Safety glasses
Ladder
'Paste-the-wall'
  lining paper
  (1400 grade)
Wallpaper paste
Brush or roller
Wallpaper
  smoother
Seam roller
Wallpaper edger
Wallpaper knife
```

1 Lining paper is applied horizontally to walls, so measure the width of your wall and cut your paper to size, leaving a 50mm overlap at the corners, which will be trimmed later.

2 Starting in the top-left corner, apply wallpaper paste directly to the wall, using a brush or roller. Paste an area of the wall which covers the full width of the wall and is 50mm wider than your lining paper.

3 Smooth the lining paper down over the paste and work across the wall, gently pushing the edges to the join between the wall and the ceiling. Use a wallpaper smoother to push any air bubbles out as you are applying the piece of lining paper. Once you are happy with its position, use a seam roller to smooth the edges. The good news is that all these tools will be reused when you wallpaper.

4 Work your way down the wall until you reach the skirting board, using a wallpaper edger to gently push the lining paper down so that you get a neat fold against the lip of the woodwork.

5 Using a wallpaper knife, snap a clean sharp edge by gently running the knife along the edges of the skirting board to remove the excess paper.

6 Use the edging tool to fold the paper into the corners of the wall and cut down with the knife from the top corner to the bottom corner of the wall to trim the excess.

7 Smooth and push down all corners and edges to ensure you have securely applied the lining paper, then leave for a minimum of 24 hours to dry out before you start your wallpapering.

HOW TO PREPARE NEWLY PLASTERED WALLS FOR PAINTING

HALF DAY/ FULL DAY

(DEPENDING ON THE SCALE OF PROJECT)

Name something more satisfying than a freshly plastered wall? I'll wait! Investing in replastering can instantly improve and refresh a wall, and although this isn't a DIY project we are covering in this book, there are several steps you can take once it's been done, so that you can tackle the decorating yourself and be sure of the best results.

Fresh plaster has a permeable finish and needs to be sealed before the topcoat of emulsion can be applied. If this step is skipped, it can lead to cracking, bubbling, flaking and peeling, which I think we can all agree is not the vibe we are aiming for.

For the seal, a mist coat is required, which is simply watered-down emulsion paint. The plaster is able to absorb this, creating a bond between the paint and the plaster. There are ready-made tins of this available to buy, but it is also a very easy DIY job that will help your decorating budget stretch that little bit further. The standard ratio is 4:1 or 80 per cent paint and 20 per cent water but check the labelling on your paint product, which will suggest a guide. Too watery is better than too thick in this case and, depending on the paint, you may need to go between 30–50 per cent water to achieve a thin consistency.

TOOLBOX

Dust protection sheets
Dust mask
Safety glasses
Ladder
Masking tape
Bucket or paint scuttle
Matt emulsion paint
Water
Paint stirrer
Paint tray or bucket
Paintbrush
Large paint roller

TROUBLESHOOTING

- Use a bog-standard matt paint for this job as anything containing vinyl or with a silk finish will end up peeling.
- Make sure your plaster is completely dry. If there is still moisture in the plaster, the paint will peel and flake.
- Protect your flooring and fixtures with a sheet. The mist coat is highly likely to drip and splash as it is so thin. This is definitely a job that requires your best (or worst) DIY clobber.

1 Use masking tape and sheets to protect any areas that you do not wish to paint.

2 Using a clean bucket or paint scuttle, add the paint (depending on how much plaster you wish to cover) and top up with cold water, using a measuring jug, then use a paint stirrer to mix until you have a runny but even consistency.

3 Using a brush, paint the corners and edges of the wall first. This is known as cutting in, where we use a paintbrush to paint a neat line around the edges of the room. It creates a line of paint so that when you use the roller (next step), the joins can blend seamlessly. Due to the thin consistency, keep an eye out for drips and blend these into the wall before they have dried.

4 Pour the paint mixture into a paint tray. Using a 23cm roller, coat the roller evenly with mist coat. Don't overload the roller as then drips and splashes are guaranteed.

5 Starting in the bottom-left corner, roll up towards the top of the wall. Move across with a steady motion, always keeping an eye out for pesky drips. One coat should be enough, but if you think it requires a second, allow the first to dry for 24 hours before reapplying.

6 You'll know you are ready for your topcoat if you apply a piece of masking tape to the surface and the paint stays intact when the paint is peeled off. Patience will pay you back in the end as rushing the drying process could affect the finish of your topcoat.

7 When you're ready to apply the topcoat, see page 120 to make sure you have the right tools and technique to finish off your project.

HOW TO REPAIR DAMP PATCHES ON A WALL

HALF DAY

Ugh, damp and mould are absolutely guaranteed to kill your interiors vibe, plus they are hazardous to health if left untreated. If you have persistent signs of damp on your wall, it is important to treat and target the original source of the problem professionally as otherwise it will reappear repeatedly. However, try this method first and consider investing in a dehumidifier to reduce the moisture levels in the room.

TROUBLESHOOTING

- Anti-mould cleaning products contain harsh chemicals, so wear the appropriate PPE, and especially gloves, to avoid contact with the skin. Also keep windows open while you work to ensure proper ventilation.
- If you are treating a large area of a wall, consider repainting the entire wall.

TOOLBOX
Safety glasses
Mask
Protective gloves
Protective sheets
Scraper
Low-grit sandpaper
Sponge
Anti-mould cleaning product
Paintbrush (size depends on area to be painted)
Damp-seal paint or solvent-based paint
Filler and filler knife
High-grit sandpaper
Mini roller
Topcoat paint

PREP IT

1. Using a scraper, remove loose paint that has been affected by damp. This will help you assess the scale of the problem. If the area is localized (on one particular wall) you will be able to treat it using the steps below. If the area is expansive and on multiple walls, give the professionals a call.

2. Sand back the area using a low-grit sandpaper to smooth the wall. Brush away the dust from the wall surface.

3. Using a sponge, wipe down the affected area with an anti-mould cleaning product, then leave the wall to dry completely.

4. Using a paintbrush, apply a damp-seal paint over the area being treated. If you do not have a damp-seal paint, a solvent-based paint will also do the job. Leave to dry for 24 hours.

5. The next day, apply filler to the wall using a filling knife over the sealed area to fill any dents and dips left from your scraping and create a smooth surface. Leave the filler to dry, then sand smooth using a high-grit sandpaper. Clean up all dust and residue.

6. Using a mini roller, paint the affected area with a topcoat, taking care to blend the paint into the existing wall coverage.

NB: This is a temporary repair — it is important to seek professional help to treat the source of damp to avoid more extensive damage to your property.

PREP IT

HOW TO REPLACE MOULDY SILICONE IN A SHOWER TRAY

Mould needs to be cleaned off silicone as, if it is left, it can affect the seal and lead to water damage. With a little elbow grease, mould *can* be cleaned off silicone. However, sometimes if the mould has deeply penetrated the silicone, or the mould is over the entire seal, it just needs to be cut out and replaced, which is what we are going to be doing here. Before you proceed, it's important to de-limescale the area you are going to be treating as it can affect the sealant. White vinegar can work wonders but do a spot test first to check its suitability on your bathroom surface. Soak kitchen paper with white vinegar and leave it pressed against the shower tray for 30 minutes, then rinse.

TOOLBOX
Safety glasses
Mask
Silicone/sealant remover
Silicone removal tool
Bleach or mould and mildew cleaning product
Silicone tube
Cartridge gun
Silicone smoother tool

TROUBLESHOOTING

Silicone- or sealant-remover products contain harsh chemicals, so wear the appropriate PPE, and especially gloves, to avoid contact with the skin. Also keep windows open while you work to ensure proper ventilation.

PREP IT

1 To remove damaged silicone from a shower tray, coat the silicone with silicone remover. Leave for approximately 30 minutes but check the package instructions for your specific product.

2 Using a silicone removal tool, gently scrape the silicone away. Take care not to scratch the shower tray or surround.

3 Remove any remaining mould by cleaning with bleach or a specific mould and mildew product. Try to avoid getting the surface too wet.

4 Silicone does not stick to damp surfaces, so ensure the joints are dry. Do not skip this step as the silicone will not cure properly if any moisture remains.

5 Cut a narrow, angled hole in the nozzle of the silicone tube and insert the tube into the cartridge gun. Keeping the pressure steady and moving in a continuous smooth line, apply a narrow bead of sealant along the join (see page 31 for detailed instructions).

6 Using a silicone smoother tool, run this along the bead for a quick and mess-free join. This will give you a much better finish than simply smoothing with your finger, so it is worth picking up one of these cheap tools.

7 The silicone will be touch-dry within a couple of hours. However, I advise you to leave it to cure for 24 hours before exposing the seal to water.

PREP IT

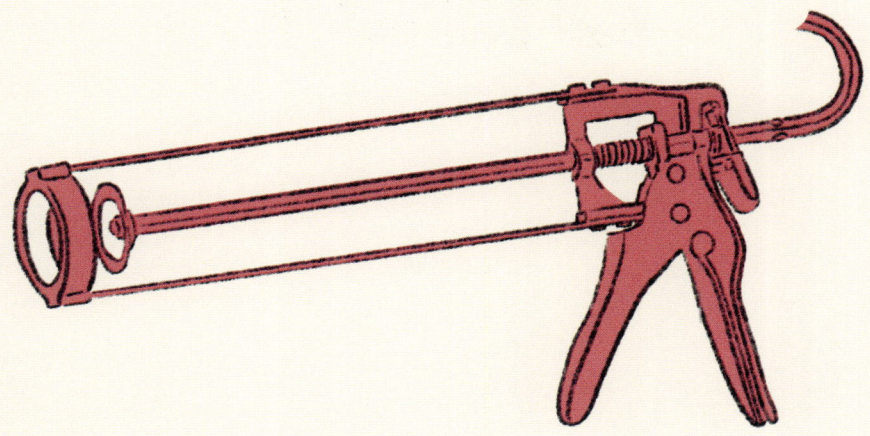

JUST TRY YOUR BEST

(AND CAULK THE REST)

When I asked my Instagram followers, 'What is your biggest DIY fear?', 68 per cent answered 'fixing into a wall'. And this was my initial fear, too. What if I hit a wire? Why does this wall sound different to other walls when I tap it? What length wall plug do I need? What happens if I mess it up? And yes, I am sorry to break it to you, but it is inevitable that you are going to bodge a wall (at least once) when DIYing your home. However, this is an 'empowering DIY guide' so here is the empowerment. Even if it goes wrong, you will be able to fix it.

Now onto build projects. Thinking of them as a combination of the individual skills you have already practised can hopefully feel less overwhelming and totally achievable. From a time-management perspective, it might take 4 hours in total to complete your project, but dividing the time to fit around your schedule makes the project much more enjoyable. Having materials cut to size in advance, tools charged up the night before and time protected in your calendar always helps.

If you feel yourself getting tired or frustrated, walk away for 15 minutes, or leave it overnight. Grab a drink (nothing too strong!) and reset your mind. Sometimes, a small break from a project is enough to bring the clarity you need to be able to finish it successfully. In my experience, the mistakes I have made have frequently been when I've been so desperate to finish that I have rushed the job, and bodged it.

Again, we should readdress the importance of wearing appropriate safety equipment. Power tools can kick up a lot of dust and debris, so ensure your eyes are protected with safety glasses and that you always wear a dust mask. Some tools featured operate at a very high decibel, so it is also important to protect your ears. Often, power tools can be in excess of 95db, so if you are working for long periods, you should wear ear protection.

BUILD IT

GET TO KNOW YOUR DRILL

First things first — get to know your drill. All models will have specific instructions, so please refer to those for your particular drill. However, they will have common features, so let's break down the jargon. If we are making holes in walls, we should know what we are doing!

Drills can be corded or battery powered. Corded drills tend to be lighter, but you have the inconvenience of having to plug them in and keeping the cord safely out of the way when you are working. Battery-operated drills require charging and then inserting the battery pack into the drill base. This can make them heavier to handle but offers the freedom of being able to work wherever and whenever!

Locate your drill settings (this may differ depending on the model). Usually there will be a rotating dial that allows you to select your drilling mode. Choose the 'hammer' setting for drilling into hard materials like concrete; 'drill' to make holes in wood or plasterboard; and 'driver' to screw.

SLOTTED

PHILIPS

POZIDRIV

TORX

1. The numbers on a drill head denote the screw function. The lower the number, the lower the drill power. It is always advisable to start low as too much power can cause your material to split, so proceed with caution and work your way up.

2. The forward and reverse button will direct the motion of the screwdriver: turning clockwise screws in, while turning anticlockwise takes the screw out.

3. On top of the drill, you can locate the gears. This adjusts the speed for power and torque (the force that causes rotation). Your drill may be labelled 1 and 2 or Low and High — check your specific model and its safety instructions.

4. The trigger will start the motor and initiate the rotation. Some drills have variable speed controls and often the harder the pressure, the greater the power. Have a play with this function before you go near a drill bit, so you learn how the trigger responds.

5. The keyless chuck sits at the front of the drill and is where you will insert your drill bit. Rotate the chuck to open it until the jaws are wide enough and you are ready to place the drill bit into the hole.

6. Insert your drill bit by clamping the shank (the smooth part) of the drill bit into the chuck. Turn the chuck until you can feel that the drill bit is secure. Some drills will 'click' when this has happened.

Now you know the parts of your drill, it is important to use the right drill bit for the right job. This varies depending on the material you are drilling into and the weight of the object you want to hold. For example, spade bits allow you to drill a large-diameter hole. Investing in a drill-bit set will give you a range of different sizes, suitable for different uses and is a perfect way to get started — add one to your Christmas or birthday list!

A NOTE ON SAFETY

Make sure you aren't wearing loose jewellery and that your hair is tied back — avoid anything that could catch in the rotating mechanisms of your drill. It's important to drill in straight, so if you need to work higher than shoulder level, stand on a step so that you approach your drill marking level and straight on. Otherwise, you risk a wonky hole and we do not want that!

GET TO KNOW YOUR FIXINGS

If you walk down the fixings aisle of a DIY store, the range of names, codes, sizes and uses can be totally overwhelming. Buying a multi-screw set with all different sizes and types, along with their corresponding wall plugs, will kick-start your project, and the list below will hopefully provide clarity on what to look out for and why. This is what you need to know:

SCREW HEAD DRIVE TYPES
Refers to the top of the screw and the shape. You will need to use a compatible screwdriver or drill bit. The more contact points on a screw head, the greater the torque. This gives you greater turning power, but also greater control when screwing into a surface.

There are many types of project-specific screw. In fact, there are hundreds categorized by material, use, drive type and size. These are the most commonly used by the DIYer and within the projects in this book. But here are some categories to look out for:

COUNTERSUNK
The head of this screw sits below the surface of the material, allowing you to achieve a flush finish. A little wood filler or putty then enables you to conceal the hole completely, if you wish.

ROUNDED
The head of the screw is domed and sits above the material. These screws are widely used in construction and the screw heads can be re-tightened, unlike countersunk screws.

FLAT
The head of this screw is, well you guessed it, flat – allowing a flush finish. Once screwed in, the head of the screw will sit in line with your material for an unobtrusive look. Perfect for cabinetry or furniture construction.

WHAT KIND OF MATERIAL ARE YOU DEALING WITH? BRICK/ WOOD/PLASTERBOARD

So now you're familiar with your drill and your fixings, you're ready to go. Ah, actually, not so fast. The next step is about distinguishing between the materials you are drilling holes into as this is another key consideration.

One of the most useful tools to add to your collection is a stud finder or wall scanner. As detailed in the Tool Club section, on pages 12–25, being able to locate your electrical wiring and pipework offers the security of knowing that you can drill safely into your walls. You cannot make assumptions as to where these are located, so do not take any risks. A stud finder also helps you locate the position of studs and joists, which can then be used to offer a firm surface to fix into once you have drilled through the plasterboard.

CUTTING WOOD

There are many places where you can get timber cut down to size for free or for a nominal price per cut. Getting sheet timber cut to your specification can speed up your project and reduce error. If you are an occasional DIYer, it also means there is no need to purchase expensive tools or risk injury. However, this is an empowering DIY guide and there are many reasons why you should learn to do this yourself! A DIY store cutting service will only make square cuts out of sheet material — no trim, no mitred corners (when wood is cut at an angle to make precise joins), no freehand shapes. Therefore, learning to cut wood yourself will allow you to be creative, to take on more projects independently and live out your DIY dreams! Here is everything you need to know about how to go about it.

A NOTE ON SAFETY

Before cutting wood, always remove jewellery and tie your hair back securely. Ensure your working environment is clutter-free and safe, and wear safety glasses at all times. If operating a machine, read the safety manual before you begin so you are familiar with how to control the blade. Ensure the item you are cutting is secured to your workbench or surface. Spring clamps or screw clamps will secure your wood, meaning you can operate your power tools with greater control and precision.

HOW TO CUT WOOD USING A HAND SAW

If you do not have access to power tools, or you need to make a precise or intricate cut, then a hand saw, or panel saw will do the job for you. Ideally, you want to make your cuts on a workbench, but if you don't have one, a table will suffice. Use clamps to secure the material and follow the steps opposite. This method will also work for cutting plasterboard or sheet plastics by hand. As outlined in the Tool Club section (see page 12), the TPI (teeth per inch) on the saw will help indicate whether you have a coarse or fine saw. The higher the TPI, the cleaner the cut.

HOW TO USE A HAND SAW
Here are some simple instructions:

1. Make sure your working area is clear and safe. Wear safety glasses and a dust mask.

2. Measure your material and mark your cut line. If you are attempting this for the first time, draw your cut line all the way round your material so you can see how straight and accurate your cut is.

3. Using clamps, secure the wood to a cutting table or workbench.

4. Use your non-dominant hand to steady your body and the material, and your dominant hand to hold the saw at a 45-degree angle above the material.

5. Make a small notch in the wood by pulling the saw back on your cutting line. With this notch as your guide, apply pressure and smoothly push and pull the saw through your material. Your speed and pressure will vary depending on your material type and thickness.

HOW TO CUT WOOD USING A CIRCULAR SAW

If you need to cut sheet timber to size or cut a straight line, then a circular saw makes it quick and easy. The rotating blade moves through the material as you guide it along your cut line, saving the manual work of cutting by hand. Circular saws vary greatly in price, and corded models are cheaper to purchase. A battery-powered cordless model is more expensive, but more versatile to use when you are not tethered to an electricity supply. You can hire a circular saw from your local DIY store, however, many large stores have their own cutting service, where for a minimal fee your sheet of timber can be cut to size on request.

A circular saw can also be used to cut 45-degree angles, which are ideal for mitred corners. The bevel adjustment knob can be changed from 0 degrees to 45 degrees, meaning you can make neat joins that are perfect for the precise 90-degree corners needed for moulded panelling.

HOW TO USE A CIRCULAR SAW
Here are some simple instructions:

1. For your personal safety, refer to the note on page 67 prior to using a circular saw. Ensure you have read the manufacturer's manual and have set your tool up correctly before starting any projects.

2. Using a pencil, mark your cutting lines onto the wood with the help of a straight edge or long ruler. Be precise in your measurements. The old saying 'measure twice and cut once' is crucial here!

3. Clamp the wood to the workbench or table, making sure the area you want to cut is hanging off the edge, allowing clearance for the blade.

4. Adjust the blade by loosening the knob at the back of the machine to raise or lower the blade and ensure it will cut through your material depth. As this varies with different models of circular saw, read the instructions to locate your depth adjustment lever or knob. Most circular saws will cut to a maximum depth of 650mm with a straight cut.

5. Make sure the locking knob is secure before lining up the cut line on your wood with the 'O' notch on the base plate.

6. Start the blade by pulling the trigger. Many circular saws have a dual safety feature requiring two simultaneous actions to start the blade. Once the blade is spinning, approach your material slowly.

7. Using two hands for stability, gently push the saw along the line at a steady, controlled pace.

8. Once you reach the end of your cut, release the trigger and wait until the blade has completely stopped moving before lowering it.

9. If you need to cut at an angle, use the bevel adjustment knob to change the angle of the blade. Align your cutting line with the '45' notch on the base plate to make light work of mitred corners.

HOW TO CUT WOOD USING A JIGSAW

If you are looking to cut out an irregular shape, such as a curve, or make an insert into a panel of wood, then you need a jigsaw. A jigsaw can also be used to cut through ceramic and metal, but this will require a specialist blade, which I will introduce in just a moment. I have used my jigsaw to produce arches from hardwood ply to transform a regular bookcase into a grander design. Other examples include cutting a rectangle in the back of cabinetry to access a socket, or replacing the centre of solid shaker door panels with boho-inspired rattan weave. A jigsaw works with a perpendicular narrow blade that moves up and down rapidly to be guided along free-form shapes. It is the perfect portable tool for creating organic shapes or cutting arches, and a corded jigsaw is one of the most wallet-friendly power tools on the market. Any opportunity to collectively share tools across a family or within a community should be encouraged, as certain tools are not needed regularly. So ask around before investing — you just never know what is sitting in someone else's shed.

HOW TO USE A JIGSAW

Your jigsaw will most likely be sold with compatible blades, however, I will run through the differences just in case you need to replace them. There are two types of system to secure a jigsaw blade into the saw. T-type shanks are the most widely used and are identified by the T-shaped base. These are best used for cuts in wood. U-shank blades, identified by their curved base (resembling the letter U), are better suited to cutting metal as the teeth are finer.

1 Before operating the machine and starting your project, revisit the safety note on page 67.

2 Draw your desired shape onto the wood. If drawing an arch or circle, see page 139 on how to do this.

3 Select the blade based on your material. If cutting wood, choose a T-shank blade. If cutting metal, insert a U-shank.

4 Only start a jigsaw when the base plate is in contact with the edge of the wood and the blade is in contact with the material. Starting the blade action before the jigsaw is fully flat can lead to the blade rebounding off the surface, which can jar your wrist and result in injury.

5 To achieve your desired shape, follow the outside of the drawn line as this allows room for gentle sanding after cutting. There is a guide line on the front of the jigsaw – use this to follow your pencil line.

6 Move the jigsaw at a steady pace and do not force the blade through the material.

7 On tight curves, you can make a relief cut from the outside of the material. Using your jigsaw, cut a line from the outside of the material and stop at your pencil line. Then continue to cut along your pencil line. As you meet your relief cut, smaller sections of material will be removed. This reduces the pressure and friction on the blade.

8 If you are using the jigsaw to remove wood from inside a shape, drill a hole inside the shape using a drill and make this wide enough to insert the jigsaw blade. You can drill several holes close together to make a space large enough to fit your jigsaw blade in if needed. Follow the pencil line.

9 If cutting straight lines inside the panel, use a piece of wood as a guide. Securing a guide piece of wood to your table and then running the base plate of the jigsaw along it, helps you to cut a straighter line.

HOW TO CUT WOOD USING A MITRE BLOCK/ MITRE SHEARS

A mitre block is used to make angled cuts in wood and moulding and is therefore perfect for making 45-degree cuts to achieve mitred corners in panelling and framing projects (see pages 104 and 173). Using a mitre block is not as complicated as you might think. A mitre block is a woodworking tool that is essentially a box with pre-cut slots that act as a guide for the saw and allow you to make accurate angled cuts, typically at 45 or 90 degrees. Mitre shears are a hand tool with an anvil base that includes markings for common angles like 45 and 90 degrees, making it easy to make precision angled cuts in thin materials like plastic, rubber, wood or trim. In the 'How to panel up the stairs' project on page 182, mitre shears can be used to cut the moulding. Both tools can be picked up fairly inexpensively from your local DIY store.

A mitre saw is a power tool that sits outside of the 'essential' category (unless you are planning on taking on a lot of carpentry in your home). It allows you to make precise, angled cuts which is perfect for adding panelling to your stairs, or cutting architrave and skirting to size. The saw can pivot to cut with accuracy – giving a clean and quick result. A purchase or weekend hire of this piece of equipment can make jobs like installing wooden flooring or decking, much easier due to the circular blade. The blade can also be changed to accommodate wood, plastics and metal! However, they are large stationary tools that take up a lot of space and depending on your particular project, a circular saw (lighter and more portable) or a mitre block and tenon saw may do the job.

METHOD – MITRE BLOCK
Please refer to safety note on page 67.

1. Secure your mitre block to a table or workbench using clamps. If you are working on the floor, the mitre block can be butted up to a piece of wood, pushing against the wall for stability.

2. Mark and measure your material with a sharp pencil in order to be as accurate as possible. Measure the longest length required and mark on the wood. The aim is to conceal the ends of the material with a seamless join.

3. Put your material into the mitre box and slide it along until your marking aligns with the labelled angle notches on the mitre box. CHECK! Does your marking line up with the correct angle?

4. Using your non-dominant hand, secure the material into the mitre box and ensure your hand is clear of the cut line! It's time to saw.

5. Slide your hand saw into the groove of the mitre box and pull back gently with short strokes to make a neat and precise cut. The deep grooves of the mitre block help keep the cut line straight.

METHOD – MITRE SHEARS
Please refer to safety note on page 67.

1. Rotate the blade to the required angle and rest your material against the support.

2. Gently squeeze the handles to apply pressure through your material.

3. Once the wood has cut through completely, release the handles and apply the safety catch to keep your shears and blades closed.

HOW TO FIX INTO A BRICK WALL

If you want to drill into brick, concrete or stone, you will need to use a masonry drill bit as this will reduce the risk of cracking and chipping when drilling a hole. The size drill bit you require is dictated by the wall plug and screw you are using, so make sure you have these to hand. If you are using a 6mm wall plug, then you will need a 6mm drill bit (a 5mm plug needs a 5mm drill bit, etc.).

You might be fixing into an exterior wall to secure lights or a retractable washing line. Or perhaps you're blessed with interior exposed stone or brickwork (a design feature I personally adore) and want to add shelving or artwork to the space.

TOOLBOX

Wall scanner or stud finder
Pencil
Dust protection sheets
Dust mask
Safety glasses
Drill
Masonry drill bit
Wall plugs
Masking tape
Screws
Hammer
Dustpan and brush

TROUBLESHOOTING

- You can use masking tape and an open envelope to catch the debris and dust, or, for the more experienced DIYer, in your non-drilling hand, hold an upturned dustpan against the wall. Alternatively, stick a sheet down and clean up after you've finished!
- If the wall plug is sticking out from the wall, this is an indicator that you did not drill deep enough. Remove the wall plug with pliers and use the drill to add the extra required depth to the hole. Add a new wall plug and try again.
- Please refer to safety note on page 70.

1 Use a stud finder to ensure there are no wires or pipes behind the wall. If the space if safe to drill, use a pencil to mark the spot where you want to drill the hole.

2 Insert the masonry drill bit into your drill. Turn the drill on to the 'hammer' setting. See page 67 if you are unsure of how to secure a drill bit.

3 Offer up the wall plug to the drill bit so that you can see the length of the plug and therefore how much of the drill bit needs to be inserted into the wall. You can mark this onto the drill bit using a little strip of masking tape and this usefully guides you on how deep to drill.

4 Position your drill bit on the X of your pencil marking and lightly squeeze the trigger. Gently apply pressure as you ease the drill into the wall up to your tape line (if marked) or your intended depth. Do not drill further as this which will make the wall plug unstable.

5 To remove the drill bit, put the drill into reverse and slowly pull back from the wall, keeping the alignment of the drill the same as when you were making your hole.

6 Clean the hole, if necessary, with a brush to remove debris and dust, then push the wall plug in as far as you can with your fingertips and lightly tap the end with a hammer so that it fits tight and flush with the wall surface.

7 Place your screw into the wall plug and, using your drill on the screw setting or a manual screwdriver, turn the screw into the plug. This will expand into the hole and create an anchor for you to hang or fix your chosen item. If you are hanging an item, you will need to leave 10mm of the screw protruding from the wall. We cover this in more detail in the 'How to hang a mirror' project on page 96.

HOW TO FIX INTO A PLASTERBOARD WALL

If you knock against a wall and it sounds hollow, then you have a plasterboard wall. These are more common in dividing walls. To fix into plasterboard, you will need to choose a multi-use/multi-surface drill bit, as a masonry drill bit may damage the plasterboard. If you can locate the wooden studs, this will give you a firmer fix to drill into and is recommended. Use a stud finder to locate these. If you are drilling into the cavity (open space) then you will need a hollow wall anchor to secure your screw. It may be a mirror, bathroom cabinet or TV bracket that needs securing. But ensure you check the maximum load of your plasterboard fixing to ensure you have a safe and secure fix.

TOOLBOX

Wall scanner or stud finder
Dust protection sheets
Dust mask
Safety glasses
Drill
Multi-use drill bit
Wall plugs
Masking tape
Dustpan and brush

TROUBLESHOOTING

- Check the weight limit of your plasterboard wall fixing (it will say it on the packaging) and be sure not to overload it as this will affect the stability of the fixing and the item you are hanging; it may also damage your plasterboard.
- Check your drill is NOT on the hammer setting as plasterboard is a thin material and you will feel less pressure and resistance when drilling.
- The drill bit can move quickly through the plasterboard when you apply pressure to the drill. Take care not to damage the plasterboard surface with the chuck of the drill by pushing too hard.
- Please refer to the safety note on page 70.

1. Use a stud finder to ensure there are no wires or pipes behind the wall. If the space if safe to drill, use a pencil to mark the spot where you want to drill the hole.

2. Insert the multi-use drill bit into your drill. See page 67 if you are unsure of how to secure a drill bit.

3. Offer up the wall plug to the drill bit so that you can see the length of the plug and therefore how much of the drill bit needs to be inserted into the wall. Mark this on the drill bit with a strip of masking tape.

4. Gently tap the hollow wall anchor plug into the hole. It should fit snugly.

5. Place a screw in the wall plug and, using your drill on the screw setting or a manual screwdriver, turn the screw into the plug. As you insert the screw, the back of the fitting will expand behind the plasterboard to fix tightly. This distributes the weight of the item across more than one fixed point, so the plasterboard screw becomes secure.

HOW TO DRILL SCREWS INTO WOOD

HALF DAY

When you screw into wood, you exert pressure on the timber as it expands to make room for the screw, and this can lead to cracking or splintering. Adding hooks to fence posts to support festoon lights, building a bench or slatted planter all require fixing into wood, but this can be straightforward if you follow these simple steps.

TROUBLESHOOTING

- Choose a drill bit suitable for wood. These have a sharper head compared to masonry drill bits, which allow the tip to grip into the wood without it sliding from the surface.
- If you are drilling into soft wood and making a small hole, you can drill quickly. But if you are drilling into hardwood or making a large hole, go slowly and take your time to avoid the drill overheating!
- Please refer to the safety note on page 70.

TOOLBOX

Dust protection sheets
Dust mask
Safety glasses
Pencil
Drill
Multi-use drill bit
Screw
Dustpan and brush

1. Use a pencil to mark the spot where you want to drill the hole.

2. Insert the multi-use drill bit into your drill. See page 67 if you are unsure of how to secure a drill bit.

3. First drill a small pilot hole as this removes wood and creates a space for the screw to fit snugly inside and so avoid splitting or damaging the wood. As a general rule, the pilot hole should be two-thirds the size of the screw. For example, if the screw is 6mm, drill a 4mm pilot hole.

4. Now fix the thread of the screw into the hole and use a manual screwdriver or drill on the screwdriver setting to insert the screw so the head is flush with the wood surface.

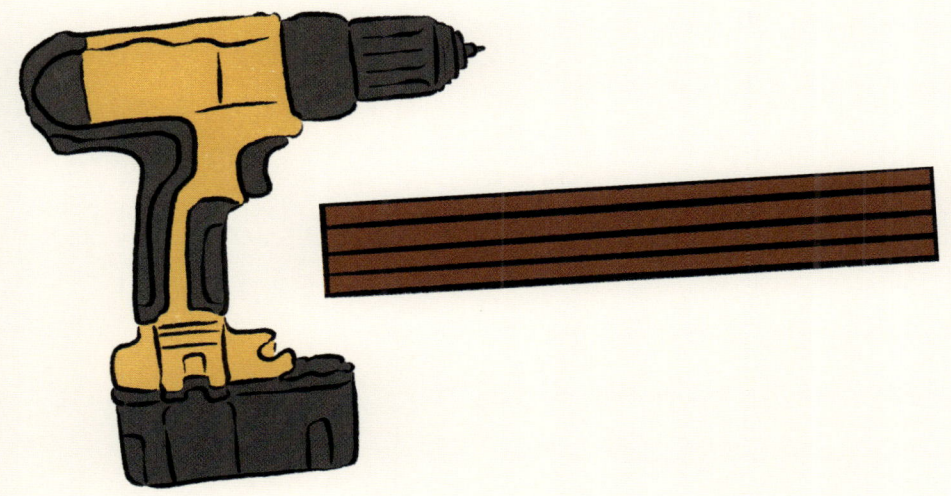

HOW TO DRILL A LARGE NEAT HOLE FOR CABLES IN WOOD FURNITURE

To make a wider hole that involves removing wood, such as when you want to create access holes in furniture for wires, you'll need a 'flat wood drill bit', sometimes known as a 'spade bit'. These come in different diameters and allow you to create a perfect circle.

This is the ideal project to make existing furniture, or a second-hand find, work better for you. Want to turn a chest of drawers into a vanity sink? You will need to create holes in the furniture to integrate the pipework. Want to hide your wires and cables? Add a hole in the back of your bedside table and create a hidden charging drawer. The same works for hiding table lamp wires or computer cables.

TOOLBOX

Tape measure
Pencil
Dust protection sheets
Dust mask
Safety glasses
Drill
Spade drill bit
Sandpaper
Dustpan and brush

1 Using a tape measure, draw a small X with a pencil to locate the centre of your desired hole. Check the diameter of your circle – does it fit the space? Will your wires fit through it?

2 Choose the spade bit to make your desired hole. The hole size is indicated in millimetres, with the number engraved on the spade bit.

3 Insert the spade bit shank into the drill. See page 67 if you are unsure of how to secure a drill bit.

4 Position the sharp tip of the spade bit onto your pencilled cross. Hold the drill flat and square to the wall and apply gentle pressure.

5 Squeeze the trigger and drill through until the tip of the spade bit breaks through. You can complete the hole by drilling the material, but it may 'blow out' and cause splintering. If this is inside a drawer or somewhere hidden from view, you may be willing to take this risk. If so, use sandpaper to manually smooth out the rough edges.

6 To avoid the hole splintering, complete the hole by drilling through the opposite way. Through the opposite side of the material, locate the centre point with the tip of your spade bit and drill through.

7 The widest part of the spade bit will appear and you will have the desired hole width.

8 If you are making holes for pipework in a sink, you will need to add holes to the underside or back of your furniture depending on the location of your plumbing.

BUILD IT

HOW TO PUT UP A SCAFFOLD BOARD SHELF WITH BRACKETS

HALF DAY

There are a few factors to consider when contemplating a shelving project. For example, the weight of the intended load for the shelf will dictate the thickness of the material and the space between the brackets that is needed to support the load and avoid the dreaded sag! Many books on a shelf can create quite a heavy load, but displaying our homewares, photos and collectibles can create a design focal point in any room. Using a scaffold board gives us the perfect DIY shelf on a budget. I have added two 1000mm-wide shelves into my kitchen and I love the timeless, rustic feel, which can be stained to be water resistant and the colour picked to suit your interiors. Adapt and customize this project to suit your space. I have added guidance on the spacing between brackets below.

You will need to use a drill bit and wall plug to suit your specific wall type. Revisit page 68 to know how to approach the drilling and fixing with confidence prior to starting this project.

TROUBLESHOOTING

- Purchase your scaffold board and let it acclimatize in the room you will be installing it in for 72 hours.
- Using a wall scanner or stud finder, check for any cables or pipes you will need to avoid before you proceed.
- If you have purchased a ready-made shelf with brackets, the support spacing will be indicated on the packaging, so follow these guidelines.

TOOLBOX

```
Wall scanner
  or stud finder
Scaffold board
Tape measure
Pencil
Dust protection
  sheets
Dust mask
Safety glasses
Hand saw or
  circular saw
Medium-grit
  sandpaper
Wood finish
Paintbrush
Scaffold board
  wall brackets
Spirit or laser
  level
Drill
Wall-specific
  drill bit
Wall plugs
  and screws
  (provided with
  the bracket)
Screwdriver
Dustpan and brush
```

1. Take your scaffold board and measure the desired shelf size. Draw a line on the material and clamp the board to your cutting table.

2. Ensuring you have safety glasses on, cut the scaffold board to size using either a hand saw (hard work, but does the job), or a circular saw if you have one (see page 70).

3. Once you have cut your shelf to size (in this example, the shelf is 1000mm long), sand back any rough edges using a medium-grit sandpaper to remove the coarse edges, before working up to a higher grit sandpaper to smooth the wood.

4. Finish your shelf by sealing it in your chosen wood finish. Apply this with a paintbrush to all six sides of the scaffold board.

5. Decide on the height of your shelf and use the pencil to mark the wall where the underside will sit. Use a spirit or laser level to check that this line is straight.

6. We are spacing the brackets in this 1000mm-wide shelf, 700mm apart, so find the centre point of the shelf position and measure 350mm to the right and left of the centre point.

7. Align the brackets with the pencil line and use a pencil to mark through the holes on the bracket. This is where your screws will go. Use the spirit level to check the vertical alignment of each bracket to avoid any wonk!

8. The bracket hole will indicate the size of the drill bit and wall plug you will need. Drill the hole into the wall and insert the plug. Revisit page 67 if you are unsure about using your drill. Screw and secure the brackets into the wall.

9. Once your brackets are up, you will need to secure the shelf to the brackets. First line it up to rest, centred, on top of the brackets. Using a pencil, draw a mark through the bracket hole onto the underside of the shelf.

10. Drill a small pilot hole into the wood using a 3mm drill bit on this pencil mark.

11. Secure the screws into place using a screwdriver so that the shelf sits on top of the bracket. Check the alignment one last time with a spirit level.

MAKING YOUR OWN SHELF

```
If you are making your own shelf, 18mm thickness will
require a bracket spacing of between 510mm for a heavy
load and 700mm for a medium load. If your shelf is 25mm
or more, you will need to space the brackets 915mm apart.
If you are using a long shelf, you will need more
brackets and to space them equally at these distances
along the shelf length.
```

HOW TO PUT UP A FLOATING SHELF

HALF DAY

Without the need for bulky brackets, floating shelves give a seamless look. They often appear 'chunkier' than fixed shelves but looks can be deceiving as they are less strong structurally and often can only support 15–25kg. (Check the specific requirements of the floating shelf you have purchased.) Also, before you start, ensure you are fixing onto a beautifully flat wall. I have firsthand experience of attempting to install a floating shelf in a period property when, despite my best efforts, the floating shelf rail would not sit flat against the undulating wall, and everything would tip forward off the shelf! Floating shelves can be secured into all wall types, but ensure you have the correct wall plugs for your wall type.

TROUBLESHOOTING

- Using a wall scanner or stud finder, check for any cables or pipes you will need to avoid before you proceed.
- Check what you are fixing into - your floating shelf rail will come with fixings, but double check that they are compatible with your wall.

TOOLBOX

Wall scanner or stud finder
Floating shelf kit (shelf and rail)
Tape measure
Pencil
Spirit or laser level
Dust protection sheets
Dust mask
Safety glasses
Drill
Wall-specific drill bit
Wall plugs and screws provided with the shelf kit
Hammer
Screwdriver
Dustpan and brush

1 Decide on the height of your shelf and use a pencil to mark the wall where the 'fixing rail' will sit. Use a spirit or laser level to check that this line is straight. Mark where the screws will go using a pencil.

2 Protect your floor from dust and debris and wear your safety glasses. Proceed to drill your holes and insert the wall plugs. See page 68 for help in choosing the right size drill bit for this job. But as a rule of thumb, if your floating shelf kit comes with 6mm screws, then you will need a 6mm drill bit.

3 Insert the wall plugs by pushing into the hole and then using a hammer to tap into the wall. Using a screwdriver, screw the fixing rail into the wall.

4 Slot the shelf into the anchors of the fixing rail. Many designs feature a small screw on the underside of the shelf to lock the floating shelf onto the fixing rail. This can be secured with a screwdriver.

5 Style your shelf! Be careful to not overload floating shelves and make sure you balance the weight along the whole length of the shelf.

HOW TO PUT UP SHELVES IN AN ALCOVE

HALF DAY

Alcove shelving can make dead space instantly useable. Made-to-measure carpentry can be very expensive, but here is how you can create this look for less using simple timber battens to create bespoke carpentry to fit your alcove space. The alcove you may have could be either side of a chimney breast, in which case you will be fixing into masonry. However in newer builds, alcoves may be created with stud walls lined with plasterboard. You will need to adjust your drill bit and wall plug accordingly.

This project will use 18mm thickness MDF for shelves that are 600mm wide.
If you require alcove shelving wider than 600mm, use 25mm-thick MDF.

TROUBLESHOOTING

- Using a wall scanner or stud finder, check for any cables or pipes you will need to avoid before you proceed.
- The dimensions can vary between the top, middle and bottom of an alcove (even in new-builds or renovated homes). Take your measurements specifically for each shelf to allow for any discrepancies.
- If your shelf is 600mm or less, you can run two battens along the sides of the alcove. However, if your shelf is longer, you will need to add a third batten across the width of the alcove.

TOOLBOX
Wall scanner or stud finder
Wooden battens
18mm thickness MDF
Tape measure
Pencil
Dust protection sheets
Dust mask
Safety glasses
Hand saw or circular saw
Drill
Wall-specific drill bit
Spirit level
Hammer
Screwdriver
Wall plugs and screws
Dustpan and brush

1. Measure your alcove and work out the batten, front panel and shelf sizes you require. It is advisable to sketch this out and write the measurements down.

2. Take these measurements to the cutting service at your local DIY store for a quick and mess-free project. Alternatively, cut the wood to size using a hand saw or circular saw (see page 70).

3. Using a pencil, mark lines on the three walls in your alcove to indicate the position of the bottom of your shelf. Check with a spirit level.

4. Repeat this for the other shelves in your alcove.

5. Cut the timber battens to size using a hand saw or use a table saw, if available. Ensure you have safety glasses on and your timber is secured to your cutting table before making these cuts.

6. Drill two pilot holes on your timber battens. If the depth of your alcove is 300mm, position your pilot hole 50mm from the end of each batten (with a 200mm spacing). Offer the battens up to the wall and mark through the holes onto the wall to indicate where the screws should be drilled.

7. Choose a drill bit suitable for the surface you are drilling into. Drill the holes into the wall and tap in a wall plug, then attach the timber battens to the wall with screws.

8. Rest the shelf on top of the timber battens and check the alignment using a spirit level. You can glue the shelf to the top of the battens using a grab adhesive, or screw down through the top of the shelf into the timber battens for added security.

9. Adding a front panel to the shelves creates the illusion of a floating shelf and hides the batten supports. Run a thin bead of adhesive along the front edge of the shelf and press firmly to secure the panel in place. You can also use a nail gun to tac this strip for extra support.

10. Once the adhesive has dried (2 hours minimum), caulk the edges of the shelf where it meets the wall. Allow the caulk to dry and paint the shelf in MDF primer. You can then paint the entire alcove in the same emulsion paint, or choose an eggshell for a more durable finish. See page 120 to decide on how to prep your shelves and choose your topcoat.

BUILD IT

HOW TO PUT UP A CURTAIN POLE

HALF DAY

Adding curtains to your space is not only going to give you privacy and the ability to adjust light levels, it is the ideal way to bring colour, texture and/or pattern into your interiors. The weight of your curtains will depend on their size and fabric type, but a heavy-duty wall fixing is essential.

TROUBLESHOOTING

- Using a wall scanner or stud finder, check for any cables or pipes you will need to avoid before you proceed.
- The maximum length a curtain pole can be without a central bracket is 1800mm.
- If your curtain pole is 1800mm but the curtains are full length and the fabric is heavy (e.g. velvet), you will still need a central bracket.
- The curtain pole you have purchased should come with the correct number of brackets and suggested fixings.

TOOLBOX

Wall scanner or stud finder
Curtain pole and brackets
Tape measure
Pencil
Spirit or laser level
Dust protection sheets
Dust mask
Safety glasses
Drill
Masonry drill bit
Wall plugs
Screws
Screwdriver
Dustpan and brush

BUILD IT

1 Measure the width of the window and mark the centre point on the wall above.

2 The brackets need to be spaced approximately 150mm wider than the window recess as this prevents light from leaking around the outside edges of the curtains. However, this also may be dictated by the available space. Using a pencil, mark the wall where the brackets should go with a small line (line A).

3 Measure the height of the brackets. Again, 150mm above the recess is desirable, but hanging full-height curtains at ceiling height can create a really luxurious feel (and can eliminate the need for curtains to be hemmed), drawing the eye upwards, which can be effective in a smaller room. Try holding them up against the window and see what looks right in your room.

4 Once you have determined the height, draw a horizontal line (line B) in pencil so that your two lines cross. This will show the bracket position. Use a spirit level to ensure your line is straight and true. At these moments having a laser level really is invaluable!

5 Offer up your bracket to the wall and mark where the drill holes should go on the pencilled line.

6 Choose a drill bit suitable for the surface you are drilling into and select the appropriate wall plugs. Using a step ladder, keep the drill

92

straight and perpendicular to the wall to get straight drill holes. Check page 67 if this is your first attempt at drilling a hole!

7 Insert the wall plugs, ensuring they fit snugly and screw the brackets into the wall.

8 If a central bracket is required, measure the centre point between the two brackets and mark the third bracket at the same height. Use a pencil to mark the drill holes. Repeat the drilling, wall plug insertion as before, and screw this third bracket securely to the wall with a screwdriver.

9 Lift the curtain pole up and over the brackets to check the alignment. Do this before you place curtains onto the pole to ensure you are happy with the position and the stability of the brackets and also, the drop of the curtains.

10 Add your curtains onto the pole. This may be by using the supplied rings or gathering the curtains to insert the pole through the eyelets or slots behind the curtain.

11 Attach the finials to the end of the curtain pole, using a small screwdriver or Allen key (if supplied).

HOW TO PUT UP A RECESSED BLIND

Fitting a blind into a window recess can dress a window with a more streamlined look. It can also be combined with curtains or voiles hung on a curtain pole for a luxurious and cosy combination. Each blind will have slightly different brackets, so it is always essential to read the specific installation instructions. However, drilling into the lintel is a requirement for most recessed blinds and can pose a few more problems. Lintels are made from concrete, metal or stone, which is a harder material to drill into than just going straight into a wall, so we will focus on getting that nailed here.

TROUBLESHOOTING

- Purchase a made-to-measure blind that fits your window space as this will avoid the need for hacksaws and fabric scissors.
- Using a wall scanner or stud finder, check for wires, pipes and wall studs.
- Drilling too hard and for too long will cause your drill to overheat and the drill bit might break. Avoid this by applying moderate pressure and ensuring you have the correct drill bit for the job.

TOOLBOX

Made-to-measure blind with accompanying wall plugs and screws
Wall scanner or stud finder
Tape measure
Pencil
Dust protection sheets
Dust mask
Safety glasses
Drill
Masonry drill bit
Hammer
Screwdriver
Dustpan and brush

1. First, find the right position for the blind in the window recess to measure the bracket spacing. To maximize light filtering, it should sit as far back into the recess as possible, while still allowing for the window hardware and trickle vents. Use a pencil to mark the correct position of the brackets onto the lintel.

2. Start with a small 3mm drill bit to drill a shallow pilot hole. Hold the drill straight and ensure you are wearing safety goggles as there is a high chance of dust and falling debris.

3. If you encounter steel, change your drill bit for a high-speed steel 3mm drill bit and gradually increase the size of your drill bit until you have the desired size for your wall plug. If your supplied wall plugs are 6mm, gradually increase from 3mm, to 5mm and then to 6mm.

4. Insert the wall plug and tap it securely into the hole with a hammer.

5. Screw your brackets into the wall plugs and clip on the blind. Again, the clipping action will vary, depending on the blind, so check the specific instructions.

6. Secure the safety cord mechanism using the provided catch. It is essential that the cord is securely fastened and taut in accordance with government safety regulations. There should be no loop, and it is advised that furniture is not placed alongside the blind with young children in the home.

HOW TO HANG A MIRROR

Mirrors made of glass can be a heavy weight to hang on a wall and so require a heavy-duty wall fixing. Commonly, fixings are located on both sides of the mirror to distribute the weight evenly, and you can calculate the spacing using a very simple masking-tape hack, which saves time and is a foolproof way to ensure you get it spot on every time.

TROUBLESHOOTING

- Using a wall scanner or stud finder, check for any cables or pipes you will need to avoid before you proceed.
- The wall material is very important when deciding to hang heavy mirrors. Concrete and brick fixings are stronger than wood, with plasterboard being the weakest. You can hang mirrors on plasterboard, but it is crucial that the weightload capacity of the wall anchor exceeds the weight of the mirror.
- Choose a heavy-duty anchor wall plug for plasterboard walls and a hammer drill fixed wall plug on masonry walls.
- Never attach your mirror with string/wire across the back. Secure using the manufacturer's fixings.
- Mirrors can cause significant injury if they fall. Ensure you have a firm and secure fixing into the wall, and that the mirror is at a level so it cannot be knocked or pulled by children or pets.

TOOLBOX
Wall scanner or stud finder
Mirror
Masking tape
Pencil
Spirit or laser level
Dust protection sheets
Dust mask
Safety glasses
Drill
Masonry drill bit
Wall plugs
Hammer
Screws
Screwdriver
Dustpan and brush

1. Take a piece of masking tape and press it across the back of the mirror so that it runs across both sets of fixing points.

2. Using a sharp pencil, or the head of a screw, mark the centre point of the 'hole' on the tape.

3. Remove the tape and place it on your wall at the desired hanging height. Use a spirit or laser level to ensure the alignment of the two markings are correct.

4. Drill through the tape using the correct masonry/multi-use drill bit. If the wall plugs are 6mm, then you will need a 6mm drill bit. You should not be able to just push the wall plugs in with your fingers. They need to fit snugly in the hole and require tapping in with a hammer. If you have made the hole too large, then you will need to increase the size of your wall plug and screw.

5. Remove the tape gently and turn the screw into the wall plug, leaving approximately 10mm of the screw proud from the wall. Depending on your mirror, you may need to manually turn the screw to make the protrusion shorter or longer to fit your mirror. You want the mirror to fit flush against the wall.

6. With a partner, lift the mirror up onto the fixings. Once you are sure you have a firm fix, then use a spirit level to check its alignment.

HOW TO MAKE A PICTURE LEDGE

A wooden picture ledge made out of scrap wood is the ideal low-cost project, plus it provides a versatile styling space for photo frames and nick-nacks! This tutorial can be adapted to perfectly suit your space and guarantees you a bespoke DIY piece that will elevate your wall — just make sure you use wood that is at least 12mm thick to ensure that it is strong enough. The picture ledge described here is 600mm long and is made from pine 12mm thick.

TROUBLESHOOTING

- If you are confident in your circular saw or hand saw skills (see page 70), cut the timber to size at home. Otherwise, use the cutting service at your local DIY store.
- If you want to make a picture ledge longer than 1200mm, make multiple ledges and join them together while securing to the wall.
- If your ledge is 600mm or less, two wall fixings will suffice. If it is larger, add a wall fixing every 300mm.
- Using a wall scanner or stud finder, check for any cables or pipes you will need to avoid before you fit the picture ledge.

TOOLBOX

3 pieces of scrap wood (for example, pine):
1 x 100mm wide x 600mm long (for the back support: A)
1 x 80mm wide x 600mm long (for the shelf: B)
1 x 50mm wide x 600mm long (for the lip: C)
Tape measure
Pencil
Dust protection sheets
Dust mask
Safety glasses
Circular saw or hand saw, if using
Drill
2mm multi-use drill bit
5mm multi-use drill bit
Wood glue or grab adhesive
Nail gun
Screwdriver
5mm screws

1. Cut the three pieces of wood to the desired length. Take piece A and, with a pencil, mark on the position of the wall fixings at 300mm intervals. Drill through with a 5mm drill bit. This is the back piece of your picture ledge and those holes will secure it onto the wall at the end of the project. We do this first as it can get a little awkward once the whole ledge is assembled.

2. Piece B will form the shelf. To secure it to the back (piece A), you are going to form a 'butt joint', where the two pieces sit together to form an L-shaped right angle. Take the thinnest edge of B, and mark three pencil crosses along this edge. To clarify, we have not marked the wider flat sides of the wood!

3. Clamp piece B to your workbench with the pencil crosses facing upwards. Drill three small pilot holes using a 2mm drill bit.

4. Now shelf (B) is prepped and ready, secure it to the other pieces (A and C). To ensure alignment of the three pieces of wood, there is a brilliant measuring hack you can use involving toothpaste!*

5. Dab a small blob of toothpaste on the three pilot holes. Push them against the back piece (A) and this will leave three perfectly placed imprints to show you where to drill next!

* If using toothpaste sounds like a bit of a faff, just use a tape measure to transfer the hole positions, but it really is a quick and ingenious way to align the positions and it can be quickly wiped away with a damp cloth!

6. Secure piece A to your workbench, and using the 2mm drill bit, drill all the way through the material. You now have perfectly aligned pilot holes that are ready to be fixed together.

If you are wondering why we haven't just glued them together, we will do that now. The screws give added strength, which is crucial for weightbearing items.

7. Add a thin bead of wood glue or grab adhesive to the edge of length B and push it together to form the L-shaped butt joint with the back piece. The holes will line up. Use a screwdriver to screw through the back of A into B. The pilot hole will prevent the wood from splitting.

BUILD IT

Continues overleaf

8. Take the lip piece (C), apply a bead of adhesive along the edge of B and secure the lip and shelf together with a right-angled butt joint. This lip stops items from slipping and will be the most visible part of the shelf, so no drilling through this front façade.

9. Leave the adhesive to dry thoroughly, ideally overnight.

10. You can sand any rough edges using a high-grit sandpaper and decide if you are leaving your ledge in its natural state, or staining or painting it. If you want to match it to your wall colour, prime the shelf in wood primer before painting it in the same paint as your wall.

11. To hang the picture ledge, place a length of masking tape along the back of piece A and mark on the tape where the holes have been drilled. Transfer the tape to the wall and use a pencil to mark the hole spacing. Check the alignment with a spirit level.

Use the wall plug to indicate how far you need to drill, sticking a piece of masking tape on the drill bit as a guide if needed. Once the tape brushes the wall, you will have drilled deep enough for the wall plug to sit flush with the wall.

12. Insert the wall plug, tapping it securely into place with a hammer. Hold up your picture ledge and secure the central screw first with a screwdriver. Repeat for the other two fixings. Your artwork/photos will hide the screws. Alternatively, conceal them with a dab of paint.

13. Now get your favourite pieces and style up your new bespoke picture ledge!

HOW TO MAKE A PEG BOARD

FULL DAY

Peg boards are the ideal way to maximize wall storage in an office or creative environment. They are practical but can also be oh-so pretty when styled with some well-organized stationery or craft items, and these days they've even evolved into statement wall pieces. When they're scaled up and made from chunky plywood, with its lovely, exposed grain, and teamed with oak pegs and shelves, they can go from utility to seriously stylish. This is quite a simple project for DIY beginners as it doesn't use a range of skills, but rather just one — making holes repetitively. It can be a great confidence boost to see something you have crafted from scratch in your home.

This tutorial is for a pegboard sized 700mm x 500mm and is made from 12.5mm hardwood ply. However, it can easily be modified to suit your needs and, if you are scaling up, I recommend you use a thicker 19mm sheet of plywood.

TROUBLESHOOTING

- Using a wall scanner or stud finder, check for any cables or pipes you will need to avoid before you proceed.
- If you are confident in your circular saw or hand saw skills (see page 70), cut your timber to size at home. Otherwise, use the cutting service at your local DIY store.
- To avoid drilling into your work surface, position your material off the edge of the table or workbench so it is clear underneath the area you are drilling into. Alternatively, use a saw horse (a trestle which supports your cutting material).
- Dowel pegs can be cut to size using a hand saw or circular saw, or simply ordered online. Just ensure the diameter matches the holes you have made!
- Ensure your wall fixings are secure, as the pegboard can be a heavy load. Ensure you locate the studs on a plasterboard wall. Do not overload the pegboard, or position it above a bed or sofa.

TOOLBOX

Tape measure
Wall scanner or stud finder
12.5mm thickness plywood sheet
Ruler
Pencil
Spirit level
Safety glasses
Dust mask
Dust protection sheets
Drill
3mm wood drill bit
12mm spade drill bit
12mm thickness dowel rod
80-120-grit sandpaper
2 x 700mm wooden battens
Wood glue or grab adhesive
Screwdriver
6 x 3mm screws
4 x M5 x 80mm screws
5mm wall suitable wall plugs
Stain or paint, if using
Clear wood sealant, if using
Dustpan and brush

BUILD IT

Continues overleaf

1. Place the sheet of plywood on a worktop, with the back facing up, and use a pencil and ruler to draw the grid pattern, with lines 50mm apart. A metal ruler helps with this: work across your material marking at 50mm intervals, left to right. Then repeat this from the top down, leaving you with a pencil line grid on the plywood. Use a spirit level to ensure your lines are straight.

2. Clamp the plywood to a workbench. Ensure the section you are drilling into is off the workbench so your drill can clear the material. Using a 3mm drill bit, drill down through the back of the plywood where your grid lines intersect. These holes will act as a guide for making the larger peg holes.

3. Turn the plywood over and secure it to the workbench again with a clamp. Now, using a larger 12mm spade drill bit, drill through the plywood, front to back, to create the pegboard holes. The method of drilling a guide hole first from back to front, followed by the spade bit hole front to back, prevents the hole from 'blowing out' and reduces splintering. Your dowel rods will need to be the same size as the hole you make; 1 millimetre larger or smaller will result in your pegs not fitting, or being loose and unsafe. To make your own pegs for this project, as the spade bit is 12mm, you would need to buy 12mm pine dowel rod.

4. Once you have made all your peg holes, sand them down with 80–120-grit sandpaper, working in the direction of the grain until it is smooth and splinter-free.

5. Eggshell paint, varnish or wax can finish your pegboard off beautifully and provide extra durability. Leave to dry, or skip this step if you are keeping your pegboard 'au naturel'.

6. Flip the pegboard over again onto the reverse and secure it to the workbench. Now you are adding the wood battens to brace both sides of the pegboard and these will lift it off the wall and allow the pegs to fit through the holes. Use wood glue or grab adhesive in a cartridge gun to add a bead of adhesive to the wooden batten. Secure with four small screws, drilling a small pilot hole and then using your drill on screwdriver setting to drive them through the batten and into the plywood.

7. To fix to the wall, using a 5mm drill bit, drill four corner holes through the front of the pegboard and through the corner of the batten. Use a pencil to mark these positions onto the wall.

8. You will need longer M5 x 80mm screws to secure through the face of the pegboard, the batten and into the wall. Drill into the wall to make the hole and insert the 5mm wall plugs by tapping them in with a hammer.

9. You may find it easier for a partner to lift and support the pegboard while you use a screwdriver to drive the 80mm screw, through the pegboard, batten and into the wall. Complete for all four corners. The pegboard should be level and the battens flush with the wall.

10. The dowel pegs can be made by cutting a 12mm pine dowel rod into 100mm lengths (see step 3). Clamp the dowel and cut using a hand saw or circular saw. Sand the edges. Insert into the pegboard in your desired positions. Push the peg until it touches the back wall, its strength comes in the snug fit, so do not load the pegs until they are secure.

HOW TO FRAME AND HANG AN ARTWORK

HALF DAY

In my opinion, every artwork needs a frame to finish off the look. This simple wood frame can be made to elevate the look of your DIY or shop-brought canvas. Best of all it can be painted or stained to suit your interiors, creating a truly unique feature in your home. Be warned, you may get tired of receiving compliments!

TROUBLESHOOTING

- If your stripwood is a little deeper than your canvas, this will create a 'floating canvas' look. However, you will need to stain/paint both sides.
- Using a wall scanner or stud finder, check for any cables or pipes you will need to avoid before you proceed.
- To secure your mitred corners and get a professional and robust finish, invest in a small tube of mitre bond glue.

TOOLBOX

Planed stripwood (the same depth as your canvas)
Ruler or tape measure
Pencil
Panel saw or circular saw
Mitre box
Wood stain or eggshell paint, if using
Grab adhesive
Nail gun
Mitre bond glue
Picture hook and pins or a heavy-duty fixing

USING A PICTURE HOOK AND PIN

To hang using a picture hook and pin, measure the distance between the hanging hook on the back of the canvas and the top of the artwork. Write this down! Find your desired wall position and mark where you would like the top of the artwork to sit and draw a small pencil line. (If you are DIYing alone, a tip is to set your camera on a timer, and take a photo of you holding the canvas in position. You can then decide if it is too high or low, as sometimes it is hard to tell when you are standing facing the wall!). Using a ruler, measure down from the pencil line and this will show you where to locate your hook.

Hammer in the pin through the hook holes at an angle to anchor the picture hook. Then hang and admire your work.

1. Measure the dimensions of the perimeter of your canvas and add a minimum of 100mm to each measurement. You want your cut pieces to be long and in excess of the canvas size, so that when you make your angled cuts at both ends of the wood, you will have enough material.

2. Using a panel saw and a mitre box, or a circular saw, cut the wood to size with mitred corners at 45 degrees (see page 76). Check before you cut. For example, If your canvas is 600mm wide, cut a length of wood that is 700mm long.

3. Lay your canvas flat on the ground and position the cut lengths around your canvas to confirm that you are happy with the sizing and the mitred joins.

4. Stain or paint the frame to your desired colour (if using), then leave to dry.

5. Secure the timber frame to the outside of the canvas by using grab adhesive or a nail gun to tack the timber to the canvas frame.

6. Use a mitre bond glue to secure the mitred corners and work your way round the canvas until the frame is complete.

7. Hang your frame using a heavy-duty wall fixing(s). Secure it as you would a mirror (see page 96), ensuring the correct wall fixing has been used for the size and weight of your artwork. If you have a smaller piece of artwork, a simple picture hook and pin may suffice. However, if your artwork is larger, or positioned near a bed or over the stairs, you may want to use a heavy-duty fixing for peace of mind.

HOW TO DESIGN A GALLERY WALL

Hanging artwork is the perfect way to add colour, pattern and personality to a blank space. How you position your prints is always down to personal preference, but creating a gallery wall can create a relaxed or eclectic feel. It involves clustering prints together of different sizes, without symmetry and, while it can look casual, there's an art to getting the layout right. Choosing an odd number of frames makes for an interesting display and is more pleasing to the eye. To achieve a relaxed but cohesive scheme, select frames in the same colour but vary the sizing. If you want to really make a statement, mix up your frame colours and materials, but consider tying them into the existing colours in your home. If you have leftover paint, this can be a really fun extra little project.

TOOLBOX

5 or 7 picture frames work well, but adjust to suit your space
Parchment or wrapping paper
Scissors
Masking tape
Tape measure
Pencil
Spirit level
Hammer
Picture hooks and nails or drill and suitable wall fixings

TROUBLESHOOTING

- Depending on the size and weight of your picture/frame, often a picture hook (commonly sold with two or three pins) will work well, and these can be gently hammered into the wall at an angle.
- Large frames that have Perspex instead of glass are much lighter and easier to hang than those with glass.
- To hang a heavier frame, you may need to fix it into the timber beams behind the plasterboard. You can use a stud detector to locate these.
- If you are hanging artwork on a brick wall, a screw and wall plug combo is best (see page 78). Measure the length of your plug against your screw as you will need to leave 10–15mm of the screw proud of the wall to hang your frame. This can be manually adjusted using a screwdriver to ensure your frame is positioned flush against the wall.

1 Unroll the parchment or wrapping paper on a clear worktop and place your chosen frames on top. Draw around each one, then cut out these shapes with scissors.

2 Start with the central print shape and position it on the wall, roughly at eye level. Use masking tape to hold in place.

3 Now add the next cut-out, graduating out from the central frame and leaving a 50–100mm space in between. Repeat until you have added all your cut-outs and are happy with the pattern you have created.

4 Use a pencil to gently mark the wall with a line that indicates where the top of each frame will sit.

5 Measure the distance between the top of the frame and the position of the hook on the back of the frame. Mark this onto the paper template so you can accurately replicate this position on the wall.

6 Gently hammer the picture pins into the wall at an angle. The angled pins will anchor the picture hook into place.

7 Once all your picture hooks are positioned, remove the paper and replace it with your picture frame. Ensure you have clean, dry hands as you may need to touch the walls while hanging your pictures. Do this one at a time. Then stand back and admire your gallery wall.

BUILD IT

3 WAYS TO ELEVATE YOUR GALLERY WALL

For one final decorative flourish, you might want to zone your gallery wall with a crisp, lined colour block. See page 134 to ensure you get the perfect paint line. Measure a rectangle around your completed gallery wall and use a contrasting paint colour that will make your prints pop.

Battery-powered lighting can also be added to your gallery wall. The section on rechargeable lighting (page 194) could be the answer to make your wall art truly shine.

Hang vintage plates or mirrors to add interest to your display. Adhesive plate hangers are available online and allow you to securely hang plates with just one small hook.

HOW TO BUILD A SLATTED PLANTER

FULL DAY

This planter build is one of the most versatile projects, as you can use numerous materials and make it to your custom size. From a small window box to a larger trough style, this guide can be adapted to suit your requirements. However the dimensions in this project will make you a planter which is 800mm long x 400mm wide x 400mm high. Best of all, it is a great project to utilize leftover decking boards, treated timber lengths or roofing battens.

TROUBLESHOOTING

If you are confident in your circular saw or hand saw skills (see page 70), cut your timber to size at home. Otherwise, use the cutting service at your local DIY store.

TOOLBOX

Tape measure
Pencil
Safety glasses
Treated roof battens (2400mm lengths x 10)
Circular saw or hand saw
Drill
2mm wood drill bit
Screwdriver
4mm exterior wood screws
Spirit level
Exterior stain or paint
Weed control membrane roll
Staple gun or hammer and tacks

1. Your planter will require the following lengths of treated roof battens cut to size.

   Length A – 800mm
   Length B – 400mm
   Length C – 400mm

   Wear your safety glasses and cut these lengths to size using a circular saw or hand saw.

2. Take 2 x length A and 2 x length B to create a rectangular frame for the top of the planter. Lay the pieces on the ground to make the rectangular shape. The pieces of wood will form a butt joint with the longer 800mm batten sitting at the front, and the 400mm battens butting up to it. This will make a neat 90-degree angle. Drill a small pilot hole through the front of length A using a 2mm drill bit. This will make the process of screwing the pieces together easier and prevent the wood from splitting.

3. Using a screwdriver, drive the 4mm exterior wood screws through the front of length A and into length B. Repeat until all four pieces of wood are secured together in a rectangle. Repeat this process again with another 2 x length A and 2 x length B, until you have two identical rectangular frames.

4. Screw 4 x length C into the internal corners of the base rectangle, before flipping the structure over and securing the other end of length C into the internal corners of the rectangular frame. Always use your technique of drilling the small pilot hole, followed by screwing in the 4mm screw to avoid splitting. It increases the time, but it is worth it for a better finish.

Continues overleaf

5 You will now have a freestanding structure, but it isn't strong at this point. Place the last 2 x length C pieces in the base of the planter. These will strengthen the base and stop the planter from warping. Secure these with the 4mm drive screws.

6 You will now have five battens left to secure into each side of your planter. Lift up the planter and tilt it so that the long side (length A) is facing up. Lay the remaining five battens across the planter and evenly space them.

7 Secure all five remaining battens to each side of the planter by using the pilot hole/screwdriver method. Keep the battens straight by checking their alignment with a spirit level, and for aesthetic purposes, screw the battens into the internal corner posts, keeping the screws in a straight vertical line.

Complete all four sides, you will now have used up all of your pieces of wood! Phew.

8 Paint or stain the planter using an exterior wood product. This will extend the life of your planter and give added protection against the elements. Leave to dry.

9 If you are adding a potted plant into the planter, then you do not need to line it, however, if you intend to fill it with soil and plant it out, then a liner is needed. Cut a 1800mm length of weed control membrane and secure it to the inside of the planter using a staple gun. Make drainage holes in the material using scissors.

10 Add some soil or a potted plant and admire your handy work! Repaint your planter every year to help protect it from rot. The planter requires annual protection with a fresh coat of exterior wood paint/stain (see page 123).

TIP
If your battens are 2400mm long, choosing a planter size that divides by the batten length reduces wastage.

HOW TO BUILD A BENCH

This bench design can be adapted to suit your size and specification. The build can also be combined with the seat cushion tutorial on page 113. This tutorial is for a bench measuring 450mm high and 1200mm long.

8 x 1200mm pieces, your bench length (A)

14 x 450mm pieces, your bench height (B)

16 x pieces (length B − width of length A) pieces (= C) approximately 400mm

TROUBLESHOOTING
- If you are confident in your circular saw or hand saw skills (see page 70), cut your timber to size at home. Otherwise, use the cutting service at your local DIY store.
- If you wish to make this bench for outside use, use treated timber and seal your bench with varnish.

TOOLBOX
Dust protection sheets
Dust mask
Safety glasses
Circular saw or hand saw, if using
Treated timber lengths
Grab adhesive
Drill
Wood screws
Screwdriver
Stain, paint or varnish

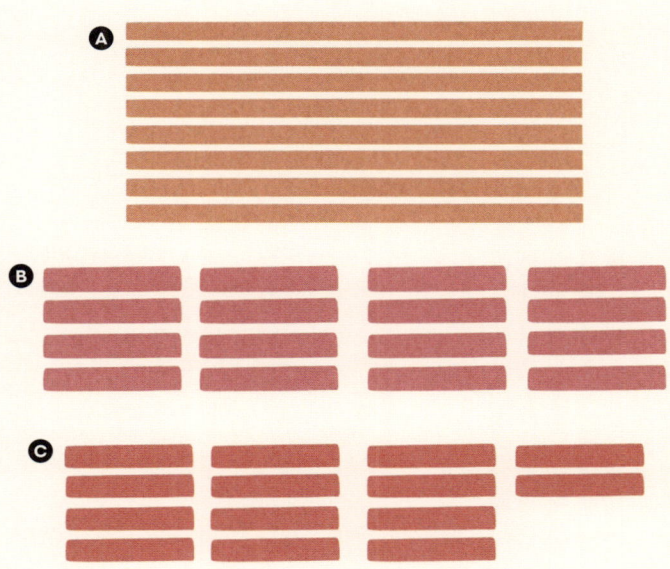

1. Lay your first three pieces of timber, 1 x length A and 2 x length C, down onto a flat surface and position them so they fit flush against each other. Add a thin layer of grab adhesive along the edges.
2. Layer length B over the leg and secure with four screws as shown in the illustration. Add your adhesive.
3. Lay piece A and 2 x length C on top, followed by 2 x length B.
4. Add four screws and another layer of adhesive on the legs. Repeat until you run out of timber.
5. Fill any exposed screw holes with wood filler and sand back the excess, then sand the edges of the wood to give a rounded edge for comfort.
6. Stain, varnish or spray paint the bench in your chosen finish.

THE LEGS WILL LOOK LIKE THIS

THE BENCH TOP WILL LOOK LIKE THIS...

HOW TO MAKE A NO-SEW BENCH CUSHION

FULL DAY

This no-sew method of upholstery creates a sandwich with layers of wood, foam and wadding and can be used in many areas of the home. The technique works on small-scale projects like a stool or a toy box, but can also be scaled up to create a statement piece like a fluted-back dining bench. Depending on the size of your project, you may wish to invest in an electric staple gun to secure your fabric with ease and save your hands from the repetition of a manual staple gun.

TOOLBOX
Safety glasses
Wooden seat, cut to size hardwood ply
Circular saw, if using
56mm thick foam block
Stanley knife
Upholstery scissors
Spray contact adhesive
Wadding
Staple gun
Fabric

TROUBLESHOOTING
- If you are confident in your circular saw skills (see page 72), cut your timber to size at home. Otherwise, use the cutting service at your local DIY store.
- Hardwood ply is easier to staple into than MDF.

Continues overleaf

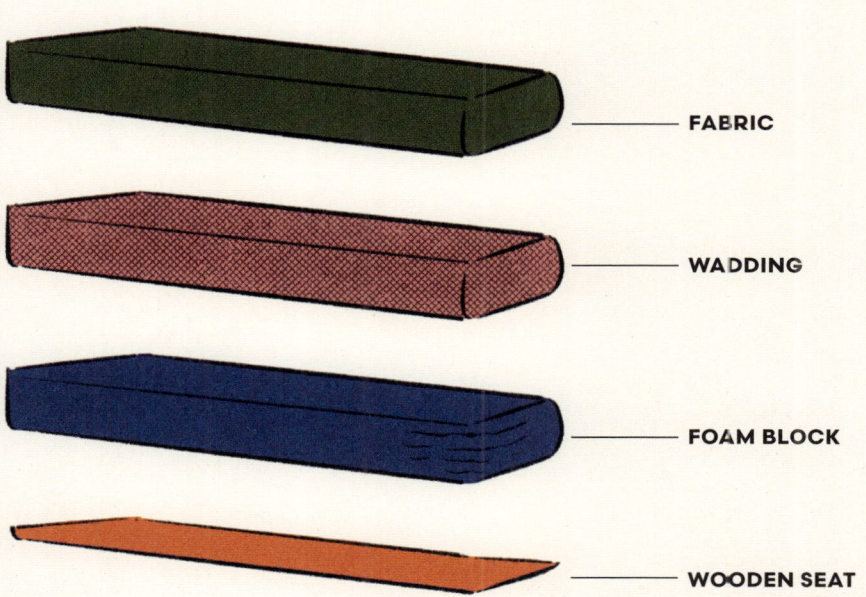

— FABRIC
— WADDING
— FOAM BLOCK
— WOODEN SEAT

BUILD IT

1. Using the wooden seat as a template, cut the foam to the same size using a Stanley knife, or even a sharp kitchen knife. However, take care to protect the cutting surface by scoring the blade halfway through the depth of your material, before turning it over and cutting from the other side. If you do not want to attempt this, you can order cut-to-size foam online.

2. Spray contact adhesive to the back of the foam and onto the wooden panel, then stick together and apply pressure to make secure.

3. Using upholstery scissors, cut the wadding so that it wraps around the seat panel and the sides of the foam and with an extra 80mm for securing it onto the panel. Do not go too small! It is easier to trim excess away.

4. Fold the wadding around the seat, and use a staple gun to secure it to the wooden base. Keep the material taut and take your time to fold the corners without the wadding bunching.

5. Once you have secured the wadding all the way around, trim the excess using scissors.

6. Lay your fabric out face-down on a flat surface. If you are using patterned fabric or a textured weave or velvet, ensure the print or pile is facing in the right direction. You may need to steam or iron this beforehand to reduce folds or creases.

7. Place the upholstery sandwich onto the back of the fabric. Repeat the staple gun process. Think about it as wrapping a present. Just avoid the triangle at the ends and gently taper the fabric to create a soft curve or a straight edge at the corners. This may take a little practice, so play with different folds before you commit to the staple.

8. There are different ways to secure your upholstered bench cushion so choose the best one for your specific project.

   A Hinges – if you want your bench seat to lift for hidden storage.

   B Velcro strips – secure one side to the top of the furniture and line up the opposite side of the Velcro with the underside of the cushion. These can be self-adhesive or secured with your staple gun.

   C Grab adhesive – can cure the bench cushion to the furniture but it might not withstand heavy use.

   D Small screws from the underside of the furniture into the wooden base.

THERE IS ALWAYS ANOTHER DAY,

AND THERE IS ALWAYS ANOTHER WAY.

In my opinion, decorating is like putting the icing on the cake – the colour and pattern sitting on top of your DIY creation. These final choices are what makes your home feel personal to you, and the options are endless! I love how colour can reflect a personality, but also how you want a room to feel. So, whether you are looking for warm neutrals to create a calm sanctuary, or the effect of a dopamine rush with vibrant hues, the techniques that will help you achieve your dream look are within reach in this chapter.

However, colour is not the only decision to make when it comes to decorating as there are so many different types of paint and finishes to choose from. With two young children, I have always favoured a tough, scrubbable paint in those high-traffic areas of the home. The formulation is less porous, which means those grubby finger marks can be wiped away as the grease and grime sits on the surface. I have found this essential on the stairs and in the hallway. But practical can also be pretty! And I'll outline all the options in more detail in the following pages.

If you're just looking for a small change, which doesn't require a full weekend of furniture removal and prep, I've also included some colour-block paint projects in this chapter, which pack a punch without completely dominating your annual leave. These techniques can also be teamed with some of the other build or panelling projects to create a show-stopping look. Or it's fine to just paint the wall. One step at a time!

Wallpapering has also continued its cyclical journey in and out of people's homes. I was late to the wallpaper party, but after attempting my first wall (and ceiling) last year, I was amazed at what an impact it can have. However, what goes up, can come down, so check the wallpaper prep and repair info on pages 54 and 55 to ensure you get your desired finish.

So what are you waiting for? Let's get messy!

DECORATE IT

PLANNING YOUR PAINT PROJECTS

There are so many different formulations and finishes available in the paint aisles — all the classics, plus new products that can be used on multiple surfaces, which can save time and money, along with specialist paints that are formulated for surfaces that have high moisture levels, such as metals and even fabrics. All this choice can be mindboggling and put you off before you even start. However, here's all the info you should require to get the right paint for the job in hand.

OIL-BASED PAINT
Oil-based paints were widely used in period homes due to their durability, dense colour pigmentation and high sheen finish. There is still a place for oil paint in the modern home, as its durability and tough finish are great to have in high-traffic areas, such as kitchens, hallways and staircases. Window and door frames have also traditionally been painted in this hard-wearing paint. However, practical and environmental drawbacks mean it is largely being replaced by water-based paint, which I'll introduce next. Oil-based paints take longer to dry and have a higher concentration of VOCs (Volatile Organic Compounds), which also makes them very smelly. This makes them less desirable to use when decorating a home, and especially if you have pets or children who need to be kept away from slow-drying tacky surfaces and breathing in fumes. With the evolution of paint technology and our increased awareness of environmental concerns, I prefer to step away from oil-based formulations. Your brushes will also thank you!

WATER-BASED PAINT
Water-based paints are a game changer for the recreational DIYer as they make the whole process of prepping, painting and cleaning up a lot easier. With their quicker drying time, low VOCs and low odour, they have revolutionized the paint market in recent years. Emulsion paints for walls and ceilings are now primarily water-based, and many interior wood finishes too.

EMULSION

Emulsion paint is a water-based paint that includes a binder, such as vinyl or acrylic resin, which creates a hardwearing finish. Typically used on walls and ceilings, it is the most popular type of paint for home decorating, especially with the ever-forgiving matt finish that gives walls a flat, velvety and very contemporary look. However, be warned that fingerprints and marks can be difficult to touch up. A silk paint finish creates more of a mid-sheen effect, which reflects light and offers a tougher surface, yet it can be unforgiving on imperfect surfaces.

The price of emulsion paint varies hugely. At the cheaper end of the spectrum are the DIY-store own-brand paint ranges, through to the specialist paint brands, which can be very expensive, and it can be hard to know whether investing more in the paint is worth it. Premium paint brands can offer a higher opacity, pigmentation and durability than cheaper brands, but I always say 'you do you'. For the quick makeovers or the small colour blocks, often a cheaper brand or a smaller tester pot will do the job, and I have often felt braver with my colour experimentation when using cheaper paint – it somehow feels less risky! But, as a general rule, I advocate for buying the best within your budget.

CLAY PAINT

Clay paint is formulated from natural clay and minerals, making it a very eco-friendly choice in your home. It is free of VOCs and solvents and is thicker in consistency, providing great coverage and making it a popular choice with DIYers seeking an alternative to traditional paints. It is also recommended for those who have allergy sensitivities, as it reduces odours and can regulate the moisture in the room.

CHALK PAINT

Chalk paint is a versatile matt finish furniture paint, which is water-based and can be used to paint many different surfaces, such as wood, metal or melamine. It gives a beautiful, velvet finish to furniture and has excellent coverage. Annie Sloan Chalk Paint is recommended for its rich pigmentation and wide kaleidoscope of colours. You can distress the finish of your painted piece by lightly sanding the dried chalk paint for a 'lived-in' feel. However, chalk paint needs to be sealed to have durability. Use clear wax or lacquer to protect your freshly painted furniture.

LIMEWASH PAINT

Limewash paint is made from slaked lime, natural pigments and water. It differs from other paint types as it penetrates and is absorbed into the surface, rather than coating the top of the plaster. This makes it breathable, solvent free and odour absorbing! The paint finish is textured and natural in appearance, but building up your desired shade can take time. Learn about its application, and also how to achieve the limewash look using good old water-based emulsion on page 143.

WOOD FINISHES/PAINTING THE WOODWORK

The woodwork in our homes (skirting boards, architraves, window frames, picture rails, to name a few) are often what gives a room its character. When it comes to woodwork, there is now an incredible range of paints which vary in sheen, and can be colour matched to blend or pop in your décor scheme. These paints are available in water-based and oil-based formulations, so it can be overwhelming to pop to your local DIY store and just 'pick up a tin'. Traditionally, oil-based paint was selected to achieve a glossy, high-sheen finish. However, this can also be achieved now with water-based paint, with the benefits of it being quick drying and low-VOC emitting. In contrast, oil paints are super-hardwearing, but take a long time to dry and emit a strong odour.

WHAT KIND OF FINISH?

You'll have a personal preference on the sheen and finish you prefer. Personally, I'm an eggshell kind of girl as it's durable, with a tough and wipeable surface, but it's not shiny and combines well with matt emulsion walls. Moving up the 'shine-o-meter', we have a satin finish, which has a mid-sheen and softly reflects the light. For maximum shine and durability, gloss paint offers a long-lasting finish to your woodwork. It can look ever-so luxurious when freshly applied, but it is also the nemesis of many renovators, especially when they see intricate features smothered in thick gloss.

BATHROOM PAINT

When decorating your bathroom, it's important to pick a specialist bathroom paint as these are formulated to resist humidity and inhibit the growth of mildew and mould, and also have a mid-sheen finish, which is more resistant to staining and water marks. Colour-mixing desks and in-store paint brands will stock the bathroom-formulated version of your go-to colour. Also, as bathrooms are high-traffic areas, it is especially important to scrub the walls down with a sugar-soap solution to remove any grime. And don't forget that it's not just the walls that can benefit from a lick of paint as bathroom hardware can also be given a makeover. See page 152 if you want to paint the taps, or page 154 for transforming a radiator.

KITCHEN PAINT

While the bathroom poses humidity issues, the kitchen is vulnerable to grease and contaminants that can mark and discolour paint. A standard matt emulsion may be too porous for the walls and ceiling and result in staining, whereas a silk finish offers a wipeable surface that may be easier to maintain in a busy household. The location of your sink and hob is something to consider. If your sink is positioned facing a wall as opposed to positioned on an island, you are more likely to experience both food and water marks. A wipeable paint finish is recommended.

As for the cupboards, a 'new' kitchen aesthetic can be yours in a weekend! Painting the doors with a specialist kitchen cupboard paint can breathe new life and creativity into your kitchen space. Alternatively, invest in a paint sprayer and take the doors outside to achieve a flawless finish. See page 128 for tips on achieving this finish.

MASONRY PAINT

Masonry paint is acrylic-based and bonds well to the often rough and uneven surfaces of render, stone, concrete and brick. It is formulated to withstand the effects of UV, water and frost, and prevent chipping and peeling. Washing surfaces with fungicidal cleaners and applying a stabilizing primer will also help the masonry paint last longer. Available in smooth and textured formulations, masonry paint is best applied with a long-piled roller for maximum coverage. A more detailed guide on prepping and painting masonry can be found on page 144.

EXTERIOR WOOD PAINT

Protecting wood against the elements will reduce the likelihood of it splitting and warping when exposed to extreme weather. Untreated wood can also discolour as it weathers, so to prolong its lifespan, two coats of specially formulated exterior paint provide a barrier between the wood and the elements and will slow down the onset of rot, although this cannot be completely avoided. Exterior timber care is essential and will need to be repeated year on year.

PICKING YOUR PAINTING TOOLS

So, you've figured out your paint type and chosen your perfect colour? Now it is time to apply it. But then you're perplexed by the multiple brushes, rollers, pads and poles you have to select from, in every size and shape and with widely varying price tags! Buying budget brushes may work out for smaller projects but they can also be a false economy if they shed bristles and affect your paint finish. The top of the range brushes, have a better level of paint pick up due to their high-quality filament bristles. Yes, they are more expensive, but if you are committed to maintaining them and cleaning them well after every use, they are worth the investment. Especially if you have multiple spaces to makeover. Here are the most popular types and where they are best used.

WHAT BRUSH/ROLLER SHOULD I USE?
Paintbrushes are better than rollers for intricate work, such as cutting in, and smaller tasks like painting woodwork. The bristles can be synthetic, natural or contain a mix, but natural bristles are best used with solvent paints, as they can swell up when used with water-based paint, making precise application difficult. If you are using water-based paints, look for synthetic bristles as these can hold an even amount of paint and apply smoothly without leaving tramlines in your paint finish.

As for the width of the brush, purchasing a multipack will give you access to everything you need when decorating. However, as a rule of thumb:

25mm brush: window frames.
50mm brush: architraves, skirtings, door panels.
100–125mm brush: fencing, decking, masonry.

THE PERFECT BRUSH FOR THE JOB

For cutting in and when you need a perfect line: angled brush.
For painting curved edges or cutting in around irregular shapes: round brush.
For painting behind a radiator or narrow gap: radiator brush.
For painting fencing or exterior woodwork: fence brush.
For painting render and brickwork: masonry brush.
For painting large panels: flat brush.

MASKING TAPE OR PAINTER'S TAPE

Choosing the right tape for your project can make or break the final result. Masking tape is lightweight, low tac and easily removable. However, it is not going to give you the crisp lines needed for stripes and colour blocks. Painter's tape is formulated to reduce any bleeding that can occur under the taped lines. Check out page 134 for how to perfect your paint lines when using painter's tape.

READY TO ROLL

When painting a wall, it may be tempting to just slap it on. However, following a methodical approach will improve your finished result, and reduce the chance of seeing tramlines or uneven coverage. Working strategically from left to right will ensure you get a flat and even distribution of paint on the wall.

ROLLERS

When you need to paint a wall or ceiling, paint rollers are easily available and come in many different types and sizes. A 23–30cm roller is standard for use on walls and ceilings, whereas a 100mm roller is perfect for smaller panels and furniture upcycles. The larger the surface area of the roller, the fewer paint lines you are going to have, resulting in a smoother blended finish. However, that being said, a 100mm roller is much lighter and easier to manoeuvre, which can be beneficial if you find it tricky to control heavier rollers.

Roller heads can be made from microfibre or lambswool – microfibre rollers will give a smoother finish and lambswool will provide a more textured finish.

THE PERFECT ROLLER FOR THE JOB
For painting a smooth internal wall: short-/medium-pile roller.
For hard-to-reach areas: radiator roller.
For using eggshell, gloss or varnish paint: foam roller.
For painting a textured wall, render or brick: long-pile roller.

ROLLER TIPS
1. Before using a roller for the first time, wrap it in low-tack masking tape and peel it off to remove loose fibres and potential 'fluff' from the roller — you do not need to do this with a foam roller.

2. Use an extendable pole, even if you can reach and access the wall/ceiling, as a pole provides a longer lever, which allows you to apply more pressure with less physical effort. This avoids both strain and the need for ladders.

3. You can buy plastic linings to line paint trays, reducing the need to replace trays as often. However, a lining of strong aluminium foil can also be used to line the tray and can be easily removed after use.

4. Once you have finished, scrape the paint off the roller back into the paint tin. You will be amazed at how much is held within a 23–30cm roller!

5. If you are planning to use the roller within the next few consecutive days, wrap the roller head in clingfilm and then tape a carrier bag over it to prevent the roller from drying out.

READY TO ROLL

When painting a wall, it may be tempting to just slap on the paint. However, following a methodical approach will improve the finished result and reduce the chance of seeing tramlines or uneven coverage. Working strategically from left to right will ensure you get a flat and even distribution of paint on your walls.

1 Assuming you have already cut in with a paintbrush, pour the paint into the reservoir of the paint tray and attach the extendable pole (if using) to the roller.

2 Dip the roller lightly into the paint and, using the ramp on the paint tray, roll forwards and backwards until the paint has evenly distributed across the paint roller.

3 Approach the wall three-quarters of the way up and roll up to your cutting-in line. Bring the roller back down the wall with firm, even pressure.

4 Move back up the wall at an angle to the cutting in line and then back down to the base straight. You will start to create a W on the wall. W for wall, or winning, or perhaps wine?

5 Roller across to blend any lines, until a small rectangular section has been filled in.

6 The key to a seamless finish is to have wet edges that overlap, so start again and work your way from left to right across the wall.

ALTERNATIVE PAINT TOOLS

PAINT PADS
Paint pads are relatively new to the market and, with a large flat surface area, are designed for applying emulsion quickly to walls with less mess and far fewer drips than a roller. A pointed paint pad has a triangular end that allows you to push paint right into corners and eliminates the need for manually cutting in with a paintbrush prior to rolling.
They can also come with extendable poles so that you can reach those tricky areas (like a stairwell) with ease.

THE PAINT MITT
Okay, let me rephrase that, the fake-tanning mitt is an ingenious paint hack that allows you to paint those awkward stair spindles, chair legs and anything a bit cylindrical with ease. By wearing the mitt, you can negotiate tricky curves and nooks with your fingers and palm. The absorbent glove gives an even coating of paint, just as you hope it would with the fake tan! This is one of those hacks that you can't knock until you've tried it as, if you've ever painted stair spindles, you'll be grateful for anything that makes your life (and project) easier.

PAINT SPRAYERS
Paint sprayers can vary hugely in price. At the cheaper end of the market are small-capacity corded tools, and these can be very useful for a home-renovation project and save you a lot of time. Paint sprayers can apply emulsion and wood finishes quickly and evenly to large areas like walls, ceilings, fencing and garden buildings, and result in a smooth and consistent finish. However, you do need to prep thoroughly as anything you don't want painted needs to be protected from the fine paint mist. It is also recommended that you wear a hair cap or some sort of carrier-bag concoction to protect your barnet! You'll thank me later.

BLADED SCRAPER TOOL
If paint has splashed during decorating onto glass or tiles, it can easily be removed with a bladed tool. Scrape the stainless-steel blade in a smooth action against the smooth surface to lift and remove dried paint splatters. Due to the sharp blade, these are an age-restricted over-18 product, so always take care and wear suitable protection.

CLEANING YOUR BRUSHES/ROLLERS
Cleaning your brushes and rollers effectively will ensure you get the most use and value from them as it means they're always ready for taking on the next project.

CLEANING WATER-BASED PAINTS
This type of paint can be removed from brushes and rollers using warm water. A small amount of washing-up liquid can also be added. Once the paint has been removed, leave them to air-dry, before sealing in a plastic bag.

Rollers can also be wrapped in plastic or you could try the 'Pringles tube hack' by removing the roller head and storing it inside a sealed, clean Pringles tube after washing! A 23cm roller fits like a glove!

CLEANING SOLVENT-BASED PAINTS
Solvent-based paints will need to soak in a solvent remover, such as white spirit. Fill a jar or container with enough white spirit to cover the bristles and leave to soak for at least 2 hours. Pushing the bristles against the inside of the jar will speed up the process. The paint will eventually break down and fall off. Dry the brush and wrap it in cling film, ready for using again with solvent paints.

HOW TO PAINT A CEILING

If you are painting an entire room from scratch there is an order in which to approach this project. Assuming you have already cleared the room and prepped the walls (see page 56), painting strategically will improve the paint finish and reduce the risk of splashes or marks on any freshly painted surfaces.

If you are redecorating a room from scratch, always start with the ceiling — there are more likely to be splashes, as you are working against gravity. Working top down in a room gives you the chance to clean up any drips, and avoid ruining freshly painted walls. Like painting walls, it's important to prepare thoroughly by sanding, cleaning the surface and applying a mist coat (see page 56).

TROUBLESHOOTING

- Protect your flooring and furniture with large sheets.
- Take care not to overload the roller with paint, to avoid splatters.
- Ensure wet edges overlap to reduce any sign of paint lines. Ceilings are a slightly higher temperature than the rest of your room, so the paint may dry more quickly.

TOOLBOX

Protective sheets
Masking tape
Ladder or step to safely work at height
Ceiling paint
Paint tray
50mm paintbrush
Extendable roller pole
Medium-pile roller

1. If you are painting your ceiling a different colour to the walls, use masking tape to tape the wall and ceiling join. This prep could be completed the night before to maximize your time schedule.

2. Using a 50mm paintbrush, cut in by painting the edges and corners of your ceiling before moving onto the roller.

3. Using an extendable pole, work the roller using the same method as demonstrated with the walls (see page 127 for more guidance on the perfect rollering pattern).

4. Once completed, rest up and allow the ceiling to dry. A second coat of water-based paint is recommended after 2–3 hours. If you have used an oil-based paint, leave overnight. Repeat a second coat.

5. Remove the masking tape while the ceiling paint is still wet.

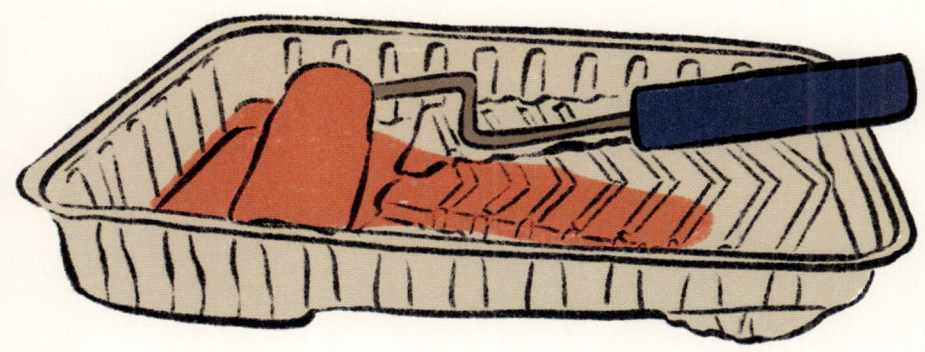

HOW TO PAINT A ROOM

FULL DAY

When it comes to completing a full room redecoration project, approaching the job in this order will get the best result and will ensure you catch and blend any drips, and can spot and rectify any imperfections as you go! Just start at the top, and work your way down to the skirting boards.

1. Cut in and paint the ceiling. This will need two coats (see page 130).

2. Cut in on walls around fixtures, corners and the ceiling line. Paint the walls (two coats).

3. Undercoat the woodwork — skirting boards, door frames and window sills.

4. Topcoat the woodwork (see page 122).

TOOLBOX

Protective sheets
Masking tape
Ladder or step to safely work at height
Painter's tape
Paint for all tasks
Paint trays
Extendable roller pole
Brushes and rollers for all tasks

COLOUR DRENCHING

One room, one colour, layered onto everything - walls, ceiling, woodwork, even radiators, you name it. This is the principle behind colour drenching, and it's a trend that has caught on in a big way over the last few years. Using lighter shades to colour drench can bring a calm and unified look to your interior without harsh lines disrupting the view; whereas a darker shade can bring a cosy feel to the space, by enveloping the space and making it feel like an inviting warm hug! Plus, If you have just read 'How to paint a ceiling' (see page 130), you may now think that the idea of colour drenching is even more appealing! Not only does it create the illusion of higher ceilings, brings cohesion and grandeur to a room - YOU DO NOT NEED TO CUT IN against a contrasting white ceiling or woodwork! I really felt that needed capitals, sorry! - AND there's no need for masking tape, multiple paintbrushes and roller trays. One multi-surface paint!

Whatever shade you go for, start with the ceiling first, following the tips shared previously. Work your way round the walls, using a paintbrush to edge in around door frames and the skirting boards before filling in with a roller. Finally, use a paintbrush to do your skirting boards, architraves and any other trims. If your trim was previously painted in a solvent-based paint, give it a light sand and apply a primer before going over with a topcoat. This will help the paint cure and reduce chips.

By using a multi-purpose paint (sometimes labelled as 'flat' or 'intelligent' by certain well-known brands) you will achieve the same cohesive finish across all your surfaces. This softens the joins between the walls and ceiling and makes your space feel more put-together and elevated. If you feel your room needs a little more texture, the panelling project on page 168 may be just the inspo you're looking for.

HOW TO COLOUR BLOCK

Colour blocking is the ideal project to complete when time, space, paint or budget is limited as a pop of accent colour can breathe new life into a room without the need to fully redecorate. And not only is a colour easy to add, but it's also easy to remove, should you change your mind in the future.

The first thing to decide is where your colour block is going. The general rule is that you are using colour to 'zone' a distinct area of a room, so behind the bed as a 'headboard' or wrapping around a cosy corner behind an armchair and lamp is a popular choice. However, you can also go for a simple and crisp mid-height line. The possibilities are endless, and entirely up to you! Here's how to get perfect lines each time.

Choose your paint so that the sheen matches the rest of the room, if you've previously painted the wall with matt emulsion, choose a contrasting colour rather than finish to make an impact.

I advise choosing a specialist painter's tape rather than generic 'masking tape' for these colour-block and striped projects — check out the troubleshooting box opposite to learn more. It is worth the small additional expense to achieve the most professional result.

TOOLBOX

```
Protective dust
  sheets
Masking tape
Lint-free cloth
Tape measure
Spirit or laser
  level
Pencil
Painter's tape
50mm paintbrush
Colour-block
  paint
Roller/mini
  roller
```

1 Use painter's tape and sheets to protect any areas that you do not wish to paint.

2 Use a damp lint-free cloth to wipe down the surface and wait for it to dry.

3 Using a laser or spirit level, lightly mark the wall with the measurements of your colour-block area.

4 Run painter's tape along the lines you have marked on the wall. Put the tape right up to the line, but leave the pencil edges visible. Smooth the tape down. Take your time with this and be precise.

5 With a brush, paint a thin line of the existing wall colour inside your colour-block area. This is the secret to getting a perfect line as it seals the tape, meaning any areas of tape where the paint could bleed, gets filled with the existing wall colour.

6 Using a paintbrush, paint the colour-block colour around the edges of the colour-block area. Paint over the edge of the masking tape. Next, fill in the rest of the colour block with an emulsion roller. For smaller colour blocks, I prefer using a mini roller. Allow the paint to dry for 2 hours before completing a second coat.

7 Using a paintbrush, apply a second coat of paint along the edges of the tape, then remove the tape while the paint is still wet. Waiting until your paint is fully dry can mean the tape peels off some of the paint when removed.

TROUBLESHOOTING

- Smoothing the painter's tape is essential so that there are no gaps where paint can bleed under the tape. Investing in a branded tape specifically for a colour block is beneficial as some tape brands have a seal that is activated with a damp cloth to produce a perfectly crisp line.
- When removing the painter's tape, pull it back on itself (not in an upwards direction) to reduce the chance of dried wall paint coming away with the tape.
- If the tape removal does pull off some base paint, don't panic. Or swear! Dip a cotton bud into the paint and, using small 'dabs', fill in the area with the base colour. Let it dry, then go again, graduating the paint over the boundary line. The dabbing action will replicate the emulsion roller and give a better blend than painting with a paintbrush.

PAINTING A STRIPED FEATURE WALL

FULL DAY

TOOLBOX
Tape measure
Pencil
Laser or spirit
 level
Lint-free cloth
Painter's tape
50mm paintbrush
Colour block
 paint/base
 colour paint
Roller/mini
 roller

Painted stripes are a great DIY way to play with the proportions of a room. Running stripes vertically draws our eyes up and can create the illusion of higher ceilings. It can also bring a playful element to your décor.

If stripes are featuring in your decorating dreams, then it's best to invest in a laser level. This self-levelling device will project a beam of light onto your wall, giving you the perfect guide to follow with your tape. It's much more efficient than measuring manually with a ruler!

TROUBLESHOOTING
- If you are aiming for equally spaced 'humbug' stripes, measure your wall or zone and divide this measurement by the number of stripes you wish to have.
- Dividing by an odd number, will leave you with a stripe sitting in the centre of your room. An even number will leave the dividing line between stripes in the centre.
- If you want the first and last stripe to be the same colour, you must divide by an odd number.

1 First, clean your wall with a damp, lint-free cloth. Measure the width of the wall, and divide your measurement by the number of stripes you would like, to give you the width of each stripe.

2 Starting at the left corner, measure across and mark this width with a light pencil line.

3 Align the laser level so a vertical beam runs up through your pencil mark.

4 Starting at the top of the wall, position the painter's tape to the right of the laser beam.

5 Roll the tape down so the edge of the tape is in line with the vertical laser beam (this leaves the first stripe at its full width).

6 Once the first stripe is complete, measure the width again and mark with a pencil.

7 Reposition the laser level so the vertical beam runs through your pencil mark.

8 For the second stripe, take the tape to the ceiling as before, however, position the tape to the left of your laser beam. You are establishing a pattern with the tape, where the first, third, fifth, etc. (odd-numbered), stripes are taped on the outside of the laser line, and the second, fourth, sixth, etc. (even-

numbered), stripes are taped on the inside of the laser line.

9. Once the entire wall is taped up, it is time to paint. As per the colour-blocking project, to achieve a crisp line, use a 50mm paintbrush in the wall base colour to seal the edges of the tape. Only do this in the odd numbered stripes which you intend to paint. Leave to dry for 2 hours. Wash up your paintbrush.

10. Now for the fun part! Pour the 'stripe paint' into a roller tray. Use your paintbrush to paint the edges of the stripe and cut in each stripe at the ceiling and skirting board.

11. Take a mini emulsion roller and paint your stripe, taking care not to roll over the boundary of the tape.

12. Repeat, painting every odd-numbered stripe until you reach the right hand side of the wall. Leave for 2 hours to dry.

13. Repeat steps 10 and 11, so each stripe receives a second coat. If using painter's tape, the recommendation is to remove it while the paint is still wet as otherwise some paint may be removed from the wall if allowed to fully dry. Proceed straight to the next step!

14. Now for the big reveal. Start at the top of the piece of tape and pull it back on itself in a downwards direction. Do not pull it towards you as this angle can lift the paint off the wall.

15. Stand back to admire your hard work. I hope you agree that the effort was so worth the impact of the final result!

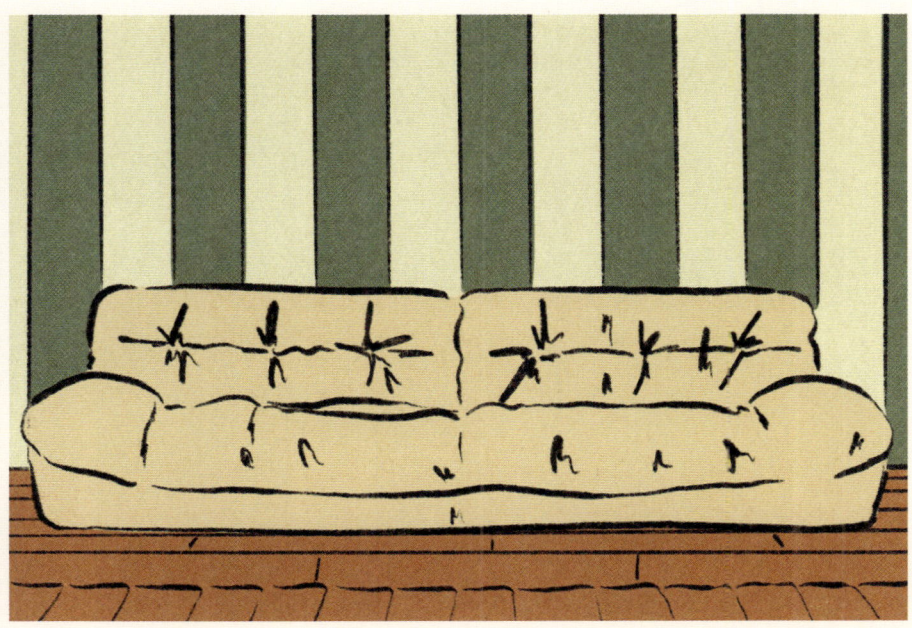

HOW TO DRAW AND PAINT A CURVED HEADBOARD ONTO A WALL

HALF DAY

Colour blocking is not limited to the square, linear shapes. Circles and arches can bring a playful twist to a space, while a series of smaller wavy lines can create a simple but interesting wall mural. One of my favourite projects is to zone a curved headboard above a bed with a painted circle. It's so simple but so effective. The easiest way to draw a circle is to use a fairly rudimentary tape measure, pencil, string and masking tape combo, or you can build a simple jig out of scrap wood (see the box opposite). The string method is quicker, cheaper and leaves no damage, but can be less accurate if the string stretches or the tape slips. The jig is more technical and more accurate, but requires more tools and will leave a hole that needs to be filled and sanded afterwards.

TOOLBOX

Tape measure
Pencil
Spirit level
String
Painter's tape
Lint-free cloth
50mm paintbrush
Colour block paint
Roller/mini roller

TROUBLESHOOTING

- Painting a curve can be a nerve-wracking experience. Do not overload your paintbrush as it is easier to add paint than make corrections to your paint line.

1. Start by choosing the height of your curved headboard and mark this onto the wall using a pencil. Measure the distance from the top of the mattress to the mark on the wall – this will be the radius of your circle.

2. With the help of a spirit level, measure the radius in a straight line and mark the centre point on the wall (in line with the level of the mattress).

3. Cut a piece of string the length of the radius and, using painter's tape, tape the end of the string securely at the centre point mark.

4. Tape the string to the pencil so that the nib of the pencil reaches the radius mark.

5. With the string taut, move the pencil around the centre point to draw a large circle on the wall. If the tape slips, ask someone to hold it against the wall, or hammer a small pin through the string.

6. Now use a damp lint-free cloth to wipe down the surface and wait for it to dry.

7. Painting a curve with neat edges can be challenging. You have the choice of freehand painting or attempting to tape the curve. Both can be tricky, but I have always preferred to freehand paint up to the pencil line. Use a small, rounded paintbrush and do not overload it with your chosen paint.

8. Anchor your elbow to the wall by pushing your forearm against the wall for stability and freely move the paintbrush 2cm away from your pencil line. Move your arm in a smooth and controlled action. *BREATHE!* Now go again, pushing the paint up to the pencil line.

9. Once the outer curve has been completed, fill in the shape using a roller. For any 'blips', use a small brush or paint pen in the wall colour to correct.

10. Repeat steps 7, 8 and 9 again if your colour block requires a second coat.

DRAWING A CIRCLE WITH A WOODEN JIG

- Cut a piece of wood that is slightly longer than the circle radius.
- Drill a small pilot hole in the wood to align with the centre point mark and another at the radius mark.
- Hammer a nail through the centre point mark into the wall to anchor the jig.
- Place a pencil in the other hole.
- As you pivot the wood around its centre point, the pencil will draw a circle onto the wall.

HOW TO PAINT A ROOM WITH LIMEWASH

Limewash paint can give your room a beautifully textured finish. The natural pigmentation can be built up in layers and it will be down to your personal preference on the finish you achieve. The method of application is distinctly different to other types of paint and is built up in layers, so unlike the instant dopamine hit achieved with applying a new wall colour with emulsion, limewash reveals its beauty subtly over time.

TROUBLESHOOTING

- If your wall has been previously painted, it will need a little prep to ensure it is consistently absorbent and ready to take the limewash paint. Limewash brands will sell a 'prep coat' or primer that is compatible with limewash. Roller or brush this onto all surfaces and leave to dry for 4-6 hours.
- Mix the limewash regularly - I recommend stirring the mixture every 10 minutes as the paint will settle quickly.
- Limewash paint is thin and potentially 'splashy'! Make sure you and your surroundings are protected. Eye protection is essential due to the high pH levels in the paint.
- Always leave the limewash to dry overnight as recoating too soon may result in the previous coat pulling away from the surface.
- Ensure you maintain a 'wet edge', which means each section you complete is blended into the next section. Letting it dry and re-starting will result in visible lines.

TOOLBOX

Protective clothing
Protective floor coverings
Eye protection
Primer, if using
Mist spray bottle or cloth
Limewash
Kitchen whisk
Bucket
Limewash block brush
Limewash flat brush

1. Apply a prep coat or primer if necessary (see opposite), then leave to dry for 4–6 hours.

2. Dampen the surface of the wall using a mist spray or a damp cloth to improve the absorbency of the limewash paint.

3. Due to the density of the lime putty in the paint mixture, this will sink to the bottom of the paint tin and requires mixing. A kitchen whisk (electric or manual) is needed to evenly distribute the particles. Proceed with caution – protect your eyes and skin from possible splashes.

4. Decant into a bucket.

5. Dip the bristles of a wide block brush into the paint and, focusing on one small area (1 sq. m) at a time, work the paint into the wall with overlapping diagonal, criss-crossing strokes to create little zones of texture. Applying a thin, even layer of paint, work from left to right across the wall.

6. Stir the paint every 2 minutes to ensure the pigmentation is evenly distributed.

7. Focus on maintaining the 'wet edge' as you blend and overlap, ensuring any drips are brushed into the wall.

8. Paint the first coat on the first day, then leave to dry overnight and add the second coat on the following day.

HOW TO CREATE THE 'LIMEWASH LOOK'

WEEKENDER

There is also a way of creating the textured 'limewash look' but using emulsion paint instead. You might choose this if you want the relaxed aesthetic, without the additional effort of continuous mixing that traditional limewash paint brings. Emulsion is considerably cheaper than limewash paint per square metre and it is also a great way to use up leftover paint. Sold? If so, all you need are two complementary paint colours. Brilliant white with a neutral shade will create the lighter limewash effect or you could try two deeper shades that are tonal and are one tone up or down in colour scale.

TROUBLESHOOTING

- Protect your furniture and clothing before you start.
- Be patient: as the colour dries, the colour variation will start to appear. You can always build up the layers.

TOOLBOX

Protective clothing
Protective floor coverings
Eye protection
Masking tape
2 small plastic tubs (takeout food containers are ideal)
2 matt emulsion paints
2 paint roller trays
Block brush
50mm brush for cutting in

1. Prepare your wall, by making sure it is clean and free of dust.

2. Fill each tub with paint (one colour in each) and position them both side by side on a paint tray.

3. To cut in, take your paintbrush and using the darker colour of the two, cut into your ceiling or fixtures. Blend the paint line down in random diagonal strokes so it softens and feathers out this colour on the wall.

4. Dip your block brush into the two containers simultaneously, but lightly, so that different halves of the brush are coated with contrasting paint colours. Do not mix the paint colours in the tray. To avoid picking up excessive amounts of paint, dipping in the bristles by about 2cm will coat the tips without saturating the brush.

5. Apply the paint to the wall using overlapping and random diagonal strokes, working the paint into the wall until you are happy with the blended, tonal look. To avoid lines, maintain a 'wet edge' by continuously blending out, feathering one painted section into the next.

6. Once you have worked across the full wall, leave to dry. If you want to add more depth to your wall colour, repeat the process again after 4 hours of drying time.

DECORATE IT

HOW TO PAINT A HOUSE EXTERIOR

WEEKENDER

Masonry paint is specially formulated for exterior surfaces of render, brick, concrete, stone or pebble dash. However, it does need to be applied in dry weather conditions, in temperatures above 15°C/59°F. If applied in cold conditions, masonry paint can peel and flake off, and no one wants to be working at height when it is windy, so check the weather app before you start! To get the best results, which will ensure the best long-term protection of your home's exterior, preparation is key. Any grime, loose debris or algae will affect the way the paint bonds to the surface, so don't rush the job – allow plenty of time.

TROUBLESHOOTING

- If the exterior is marked with stubborn stains, use a pressure washer to treat it with a fungicidal solution for masonry (available from DIY stores) or make your own bleach solution (10 parts water: 1 part bleach), then rinse off with clean water. However, take care to protect soil from any chemical run-off when using cleaning products outside.
- For textured paint, use a short-pile roller.

TOOLBOX

Safety glasses
Protective clothing and sheets
Stiff brush
Block brush
Exterior filler and knife, if using
Sandpaper
100mm flat brush
Masonry primer
Masonry paint
30cm masonry roller
Extendable pole

1 Use a stiff brush to remove dust and loose debris from the building's exterior. Alternatively, use a pressure washer to remove stubborn stains (see above). Leave to dry completely – the paint will not bond to a damp surface, so try to work on a dry, sunny day.

2 Fill any holes or cracks with an exterior filler as these have been formulated to withstand temperature changes and moisture. For small cracks, apply using a filler knife, or use a pointing tool for larger areas. If the hole is greater than 12mm deep, you will need to layer the filling, so leave overnight to dry and then add

Continues overleaf

another layer. Once dry, sand and smooth with low-grit sandpaper, working up to a high grit for a smooth finish. Attempt to match the texture of the rest of the wall.

3. Apply a masonry primer. This is optional but, as with any primer, it improves the coverage of the topcoat and can provide extra durability as a defence against the elements. Cut in with your 100mm flat brush, before applying the primer with the roller. Leave the primer to dry for 3—5 hours in temperatures above 20°C/68°F, or longer if it is cooler.

4. Clean your brushes and roller head and leave to air dry.

5. Pour some masonry paint into a pail and use the masonry brush to cut in your edges, corners and around any tricky obstacles like windows and doors.

6. Using a 30cm masonry roller (which typically has a longer pile to hold more paint and deal with the texture of the surface) start at the top and work your way down until the wall is covered.

7. Leave the first coat to dry. It is important that it has enough time to dry for the recommended number of hours specified on the paint tin.

8. The coverage may possibly be looking good after just one coat, but a second is essential to completely protect the exterior surface. Do not be tempted to skip this as it may affect the longevity of your paint job.

ALTERNATIVE METHOD

It is also possible to spray-paint masonry. This requires the surface preparation of step one, but with the additional task of masking and protecting all other surfaces. The spraying technique is quicker on simple jobs like painting a brick wall. But for tasks where there are lots of doors, windows, soffits and facias to navigate and neighbours/cars in close proximity, you may find it easier and safer to use the brush and roller method. You can read more about paint sprayers on page 128.

HOW TO PAINT A UPVC DOOR

HALF DAY

(x 2, TO ALLOW FOR DRYING TIME)

If you have fallen out of love with the exterior of your home or are looking for some fresh kerb appeal, painting your UPVC windows or door can give it an instant facelift! Choosing a new colour is also your chance to project a glimpse of your interiors personality to the wider world. Will you choose a pop of colour, dark or opt for a muted neutral? There are many new paint formulations on the market for composite and PVC surfaces that offer a tough and durable finish. All you need is a little prep and some dry weather.

TOOLBOX

Protective sheets
Masking tape
Safety glasses
Sugar soap
Sponge
220-grit sandpaper
Primer
UPVC specialist paint
Foam roller/paint sprayer/paintbrush
Angled paintbrush to aid cutting in, if using

TROUBLESHOOTING

- Time this project carefully! Don't attempt it in the winter months as the temperature needs to be above 10°C/50°F and dry for 48 hours after painting. Direct sunlight, temperatures exceeding 32°C/90°F, pets, children and clumsy adults also all need to be kept out of the way!
- Most of the paint brands claim their UPVC paint formulations are self-sealing and UV-resistant, but you are advised to avoid contact with the surfaces for a further 48 hours after painting. It can take up to three weeks for the paint to fully harden and cure.

1 Exterior surfaces get incredibly grimy, so clean the surface thoroughly with sugar soap solution and a sponge, before rinsing with clean water. Do not rush this part as any residue left on the door will affect the longevity of the paint finish.

2 Remove any hardware or cover with protective tape.

3 Using a 220-grit paper, lightly sand the UPVC surface. This will help provide a 'key' for the paint to adhere to. Clean the surface of dust and ensure it is dry.

4 Some brands of paint claim to be 'self-priming'. If this is the case, you can go straight in with your topcoat. However, I think a coat of primer (such as Zinsser Bullseye 1-2-3) can

Continues overleaf

only extend the life of the finish, and especially with the unpredictable nature of the weather these days!

5. Paint with the door open so you can access the whole façade. If you are painting both sides of the door, this also gives you the opportunity to paint the other side while one dries.

6. Now choose your technique. Will you use a paint sprayer or a paintbrush? A paint sprayer gives an even coverage and will be quicker in its execution, but you will need to ensure you cover and protect all surrounding brickwork, glass and hardware first. As these paints are self-levelling, a paintbrush can also give a lovely result. Use a 25mm paintbrush to cut in around any door hardware, then use a small foam roller on doors with a wider flat area. Paint in the direction of the grain or panel. Leave to dry for 2 hours.

7. When the first coat is dry, apply a second coat and remove any protective tape before the paint has fully dried.

8. Before you reattach any removed hardware, it might be a good opportunity to clean them up. Consider making a thick paste of bicarbonate of soda with a tiny dash of lemon juice, coating the hardware for 30 minutes before rinsing clean in warm water with a Brillo pad. Alternatively, try using Brasso, buffing it into the hardware in circular motions and dry with a soft cloth.

9. Enjoy the admiring looks you get from the neighbours and smile every time you come home!

HOW TO PAINT A WOODEN INTERNAL DOOR

To achieve a professional-looking paint finish on a wooden door, it is easier to take the door off its hinges and rest across two trestles rather than paint in situ. This will give you access to all edges of the door. If your door is already painted or varnished, you have two choices based on the condition of your door and your time/budget allowance.

a) Strip the door to remove the existing layers of topcoat. See page 34 on stripping wood. Once your door is clean, dry and dust-free, apply a wood primer to the door using a brush, before leaving to dry.

b) If you just want to refresh the paintwork, clean the door and apply a coat of undercoat with a brush and mini foam roller, before leaving to dry.

For the topcoat, choose a durable but matt eggshell paint or if you prefer a softer sheen, satin paint. Page 122 can help you decide which finish is best for you.

Paint your door in this order - PRIMER/UNDERCOAT/TOPCOAT.

Using a brush, paint the outside edges of the door first before painting the inside of any panels the door may have. Continue painting any vertical panels in the door from top to bottom, before working on the horizontal parts of the door. Blend where the painted areas meet each other, ensuring there is no build-up of paint. Finally, complete the outer verticals of the door.

HOW TO PAINT TILES

(x 2, TO ALLOW FOR DRYING TIME)

Painting tiles can be a cost-effective way to give your bathroom or hall flooring a revamp without the expense and disruption of replacing them. New tile paint formulations are durable and water-resistant, so it just takes a little prep to get them looking like new!

TOOLBOX
Protective sheets
Masking tape
Safety glasses
Plastic gloves
Sugar soap
Sponge
Small paintbrush
Mini foam roller
Tile paint
Grout pen, if using
Matt tile sealant, if using

TROUBLESHOOTING
- You may wish to wear safety glasses or gloves to keep the robust paint off your skin.
- Tile paint is thicker than other types of paint, so avoid drips and brush marks by painting in a well-lit environment.
- Keep your working space well ventilated.

1. Use masking tape and sheets to protect any areas that you do not wish to paint.

2. Clean the old tiles thoroughly with sugar soap to ensure that no existing grime or residue affects the bond between the paint and the tiles. Allow to dry completely.

3. Using a small brush, apply the paint over the grout lines first. Paint in straight lines to gently work the product into the grout.

4. Using a mini foam roller, apply the paint over the rest of the tiles to ensure you smooth out any brush marks. Leave to dry for 2 hours.

5. When dry, apply a second coat using the foam roller.

6. If you want to have a contrasting grout line, use a grout pen to draw a line over the grout (if using).

7. Most tile paints will say they do not require sealing. However, if your tiles are in a high-traffic area (like a hallway) or in a place with high moisture levels (like a bathroom), then a clear matt sealant will add a protective layer to the paint finish.

ALTERNATIVE METHOD
You can add a stencil design on top of the base colour, but ensure you use a tile-specific paint for this too.

HOW TO PAINT A TAP

(x 2, TO ALLOW FOR DRYING TIME)

Yes, you can paint a tap! If you're over chrome, or regret your black fixtures, it is possible to give them an update without calling out the plumber. The longevity of this paint project will depend on the prep and level of use it receives. But it can be a great short- to medium-term solution for your bathroom or kitchen. Safety glasses and a mask will help protect you from the airborne paint particles.

TOOLBOX
```
Protective sheets
Masking tape
240-grit sandpaper
Painter's tape
Metal primer
Metal spray paint
White spirit
Clear laquer, if
  using
```

1 Use masking tape and sheets to protect any areas that you do not wish to paint.

2 Sand the tap! A sentence rarely said, but rubbing the surface of your tap with a high-grit sandpaper will scuff and dull the shine of the existing tap surface. This will provide a key for the primer and paint to bond to and reduce chips and the paint lifting.

3 Clean the tap and surrounding area and remove any dust or particles from the sanding. Once completely dry, use painter's tape to carefully barrier the surrounding sink and tiles. The 'tape and drape' ready-roll sheets are great as they provide a polythene protection sheet that can cover walls and floors. Do not rush this stage as those pesky paint particles will find a way through any holes or seams in your protective layer.

DECORATE IT

4. Use a metal primer spray paint and after thoroughly shaking the can as per the product instructions, lightly mist the tap with the primer spray. When spraying, keep the product moving with light stokes from different directions. Leave to dry. At this point you will notice any imperfections which can be re-sanded, and a second thin layer of primer added.

5. Pick your topcoat spray paint. Ensure it is suitable for metal. A satin finish will have more shine to it and a matt will give you a flat finish. Watermarks are more noticeable on matt surfaces, but choose a finish to suit you.

6. Using light strokes in different directions, spray the topcoat over the tap. Avoid one thick coat to prevent paint runs and keep your hand moving freely while applying the paint. The longer you leave the paint to cure, the better the finish. If you can, put a 'no entry' sign on the bathroom door and leave overnight.

7. Remove the tape and sheet protection. Spoiler alert – you are likely to have an area where the paint particles have landed or fallen outside of the tap. On tile and ceramic, this can be removed quickly with white spirit. For small areas, use a cotton bud to reach the nooks and crannies.

8. An optional spray of clear lacquer provides an extra-tough finish but will require another 24 hours of drying time.

HOW TO PAINT A RADIATOR

HALF DAY

(x 2, TO ALLOW FOR DRYING TIME)

Painting a radiator is a fantastic way to embrace the colour-drenching trend or update the look and finish of an old rad.

TOOLBOX
Protective sheets
Masking tape
Dust mask
Sandpaper
Metal primer
50mm paintbrush
Specialist radiator paint/ alternative topcoat

TROUBLESHOOTING
Radiators need to be turned off for this job, so this project is best suited to the warmer months of the year.

1. Use masking tape and sheets to protect any areas that you do not wish to paint.

2. Make sure the radiator is off and will not come back on in the 24 hours after painting as this would affect the adhesion of the paint on the surface.

3. Clean! Radiators are notoriously dusty, so vacuum thoroughly and remove any hair and dirt from the radiator. Remove grease and grime by wiping with a damp cloth. Leave to dry.

4. Use a low-grit sandpaper and by hand, remove any rust marks or rough sections before increasing the grit to smooth over. Clean again.

5. There are lots of 'radiator paints' on the market that are formulated to form a durable bond to metal and withstand the heating and cooling of a radiator. You can also use a regular eggshell or emulsion paint if you apply a metal primer first.

6. Using a 50mm brush, paint the edges of the radiator first before working down in long strokes into the grooves. Work across with vertical strokes, blending each wet painted section with the next for a seamless finish and fewer or preferably no brush lines.

7. Once you have painted one full coat, leave to dry for 24 hours before repeating again for a second coat. Dependent on the paint shade, decide if you need a third.

8. Radiator pipes can also be painted using the same products, but ensure the valves are not painted over as this can seal them shut! Alternatively, adding pipe collars is a cost-effective way to instantly transform your pipes.

9. Avoid turning the heating on for 2 days to allow the paint to cure fully.

TOP TIP
Remove stubborn rust marks from a radiator by rubbing a ball of aluminium foil in a circular motion over the rust spot.

HOW TO MAKE TEXTURED ARTWORK

QUICK & QUIET

Large pieces of art are expensive, and it can be hard to find the perfect thing to suit your space, so why not try to make your own. Even if your fine-art skills are a little more pre-school than Picasso, that does not matter when you are working on texture! From personal experience, I struggle to draw with any sense of proportion but found my flair with the filler! And you can too...

TROUBLESHOOTING
Think about your design beforehand. You can seek inspiration and use other artworks for reference and sketch out ideas on a piece of paper.

TOOLBOX
Protective sheets
Canvas (size to fit your desired wall space)
Pencil
Ready-mixed filler
Filler knife
Scraping tools, if using
Painter's tape, if using

1. Create a clean, clear workspace and set your canvas in front you on a table or easel. You can freestyle your design straight onto the canvas, but I like to use a pencil to lightly mark my abstract design onto the canvas.

2. Apply the ready-mixed filler onto the canvas using a filler knife. Now this is where you can get as creative as you like — pushing, smearing, smoothing and pressing the filler onto the canvas until you are happy with your design.

3. If you like, you can use other tools to create additional texture and patterns. Plastic sculpture tools (cost-effective and available online) are good for scoring curved lines and grooves into the filler. Or you could use painter's tape for painting crisp, abstract lines. The bicarbonate paint hack (see page 200) would also bring texture to your canvas, or you could create lines with a hot glue gun, which are also paintable.

4. Once your masterpiece is dry, leave it au naturel for a minimalist vibe or add colour with paint. Leftover decorating paint will tie your artwork in with the colour palette of your home, but if using matt emulsion, use thin coats as otherwise the paint will crack.

5. Now turn to pages 208–211 to elevate your masterpiece with a bespoke frame.

TOP TIP
Check out your local charity shop as you might be able to pick up an art canvas there.

DECORATE IT

HOW TO PAINT FABRIC

HALF DAY

(x 2, TO ALLOW FOR DRYING TIME)

With our home décor schemes, we can often feel tied to a particular colour because of the large pieces of furniture we have invested in, like a sofa or an armchair. However, some fabric pieces can be updated with paint, which is much more cost-effective than reupholstering! Specific upholstery paint brands, like Fabricoat, sell fabric paint in a range of colours, or you can even make your own (see page 158), which allows you to create exactly the tone you are after. However, for durability, using a branded upholstery paint is recommended.

TOOLBOX

Protective sheets
Masking tape
Misting spray bottle
50mm paintbrush
Fabric paint
Soft bristled brush

TROUBLESHOOTING

- Your fabric needs to be lighter than the paint colour you are applying to achieve the best result.
- Blending a wet edge will allow you to seamlessly join each section of your painting.
- Velvet and plush fabrics have a larger surface area and will require more paint and work to achieve the same coverage.
- The absorbency of the fabric and the paint colour you choose will affect the coverage and result, so it is difficult to write a guide that covers all paint and fabric combinations! If it is looking patchy, paint another coat. If it is looking stiff, dry brush it again. Most importantly, do not use your refreshed furniture until you are 100 per cent sure it is bone dry.

1. Use sheets and masking tape to protect any areas of the item of furniture that you do not wish to paint.

2. It is advisable to test the paint before you commit to the whole project. Choose a small patch of fabric on a hidden part of the furniture.

3. Dampen the fabric with water using a misting bottle. Starting with a small area, dip a 50mm paintbrush into the paint and paint over the fabric, working the brush in different directions to push the paint into the pile.

4. As the paint is drying, use a soft bristled brush to 'dry-brush' the furniture. This loosens the fibres and stops it from drying stiff and crispy.

5. Leave to dry for 2–4 hours before attempting a second coat. You do not need to mist for the second coat.

6. Leave the chair or sofa for 24 hours before dry-brushing it once more to make the fabric softer and more tactile.

HOW TO PAINT FURNITURE WITH DIY FABRIC PAINT

Making your own fabric paint is a budget-boosting way to reinvent your furniture. The other benefit to making your own formulation is that you can choose a paint colour you already have and love, and are not limited to the range offered by shop-bought fabric paint.

TROUBLESHOOTING

- Mixing the fabric conditioner, paint and water can be messy, as the liquids all have a different consistency. Persist until you have a smooth mixture with even colour pigments. This will ensure you get an even colour distribution in your paint.
- Using a spray bottle can result in the surrounding flooring getting wet and slippery. Protect your flooring and clothing before you start.

TOOLBOX

Protection for flooring and clothing
Plastic container to hold the mixture
Fabric conditioner
Emulsion paint or acrylic paint in your chosen colour
Paint mixing stick/old wooden spoon
Misting spray bottle

1. In a container, mix 1 part water with 1 part fabric conditioner and 2 parts paint.

2. Mix thoroughly, stirring until you have a smooth but runny consistency. This mixture will start to separate if left, so continuously stir to ensure the pigment and texture remain consistent. Pour into the spray bottle.

3. Your furniture will require up to three coats, particularly if you are significantly changing the fabric colour.

4. Once dry, buffing the dry paint will restore softness and loosen the fabric fibres.

HOW TO HANG WALLPAPER

FULL DAY

Currently, wallpaper is riding a wave of popularity, and the range of colours, patterns and murals to suit all budgets and interior styles makes it one of the must-have DIY skills to acquire. Whether you are wallpapering a whole room, a feature wall, a half wall above panelling or you are braving the fifth wall (the ceiling) for the first time, here's all you need to get started. And if you're like me, once you have completed one wallpaper project, you'll be eyeing up your next!

TOOLBOX
Wallpaper
Wallpaper adhesive
Pencil
Ruler
Spirit or laser level
100mm paint roller
50mm paintbrush
Wallpaper hanging kit:
Retractable knife
Seam roller
Edging tool
Soft-bristled brush
Sponge

TROUBLESHOOTING

- Before you start, read 'How to prep your wall for wallpapering' on page 54, to ensure you achieve a professional-looking finish.
- Choosing a 'paste-the-wall' type of wallpaper will make your DIY life a lot easier than the traditional 'paste-the-paper' options. You won't need a pasting table and you'll save yourself a lot of mess!
- Each roll of wallpaper will have a batch number on it. Be sure to order all the paper you require at the same time as there could be slight colour or print discrepancies between different batches.

1. Measure the wall you are going to paper and use this simple calculation to work out how much wallpaper you are going to need:

   Wall width x wall height = X metres squared

   X metres squared + 10% for trimming and wastage = amount of wallpaper required

   If a wall includes an obstacle, like a window or door, measure the obstacle in metres squared and subtract this calculation from the total above.

2. Prep the walls and unscrew sockets. Loosen the socket screws but do not completely disconnect the socket without a qualified electrician. Loosening the screws will give you a few millimetres of clearance, which is enough to make cuts around the socket before screwing it back into position.

3. Using a pencil, ruler and spirit level, draw a 'plumb line' 500mm from the edge of the wall. This will give you a precise vertical reference line for hanging the wallpaper straight, so don't start from the corner as this is most likely not straight. Most

papers are around 530mm wide, so this provides a little excess to trim at the end. Getting the first line right will mean the rest can follow the same alignment and avoid the dreaded wonk!

4 Cut the first drop to size, allowing at least 100mm of extra paper for trimming.

5 Using a paint roller, apply the wallpaper adhesive (either bought ready-mixed for ease or made from paste granules and water as per the instructions), to the wall, a little wider (25mm) than the plumb line. Use a smaller paintbrush to ensure the paste gets into the corners and right to the skirting board line.

Continues overleaf

6. Lift your wallpaper to the top of your wall and allow 30mm overhang. Check the alignment with the plumb line and slowly smooth from the centre to the edges to remove any bubbles or wrinkles. Use a wallpaper smoother with light, even pressure to ensure you do not stretch the paper.

7. Working to the right of the first section of wallpaper, paste the wall with adhesive and align the next drop, ensuring at least 30mm of overhang at the ceiling. Again, using the smoother, push air bubbles out and slide the paper to meet the adjoining drop.

8. Remove any excess paste with a clean sponge and apply a wallpaper seam roller to the edges to ensure they are, well, seamless. Continue this all the way along the wall until you meet a corner.

9. Using a wallpaper smoother, push the paper into the bottom of the skirting board and into the corner of the wall. This will create a crease or gentle 'corner fold'. Peel back the paper, and at an angle, cut from the outside edge of the paper to this fold with sharp scissors. Scissors are used rather than a knife for this angled cut as the paper is wet with adhesive and when peeled away from the wall, a knife may drag or rip the paper.

10. Smooth the paper back down to the wall. You will now have two clear edges to trim using the wallpaper knife on both sides of the corner. Be sure to 'snap' a new blade for this to get a clean cut.

WALLPAPERING AROUND A SOCKET

Use a paintbrush to apply wallpaper adhesive around the socket, then gently press the paper down and feel for the edges of the socket plate. This pressure will leave indentations in the wallpaper as a guide.

Carefully puncture or cut into the middle of the indentations, being careful not to mark or scratch your hardware.

Using scissors, cut to the corners of the indentation and fold them back. Press the edges of the wallpaper down.

Snap the wallpaper knife so you have a sharp blade and cut around the socket.

Tighten the screws on your socket and continue with the next wallpaper drop.

USEFUL HACKS FOR REPAIRING WALLPAPER

Accidents happen, especially when pets and children are involved, and wallpaper can sometimes lift or tear over time. Fear not, you do not need to fully redecorate! Assess the damage and try these simple techniques to patch and repair your wallpaper.

IF YOU HAVE A SMALL RIP/TEAR IN THE SEAM OF THE PAPER:
Using a small brush or cotton bud, gently reapply wallpaper adhesive behind the damaged section. Apply pressure to smooth the paper back down and use a seam roller to eliminate air bubbles and reduce the visible edges. Wipe additional adhesive away using a damp, clean sponge.

IF YOU HAVE DAMAGE IN THE MIDDLE OF A WALLPAPER DROP:
Sellotape is the nemesis of a wallpapered room as it often removes just the top printed layer of the paper, leaving a light surface rip visible. However, if you have an offcut of the wallpaper left, all is not lost! Cut out a small section of wallpaper to match the exact size of the rip. If there is a large pattern in the paper (for example, a flower) then cut round the entire flower. Using a small brush apply wallpaper adhesive to the cutout and then smooth the shape back down, using a seam roller to press out wrinkles and blend the edges. Depending on your lighting or the position of this 'patch', it should be a little secret that only you know!

IF YOUR WALLPAPER IS LIFTING:
If your wallpaper drop is peeling at the corners or lifting at the bottom, it may mean a couple of things.
1) Poor adhesion between the paper and the wall
2) Excess moisture or damp in the wall.

If it is issue 1, then it is easily fixed by applying more adhesive paste to the wall, brushing your paper down and using a smoothing tool to push out the air bubbles.

If you suspect it is issue 2, then papering over the damp again is just pushing your problem to a later date. You will need to locate the source of the damp problem, dry the wall out and repaint in a damp-proof emulsion paint. Once this has been achieved, wallpaper can be reapplied to the wall.

DECORATE IT

Panelling is having an absolute moment in interior design and is one of the best ways to bring character to your walls. And, as panelling has been adorning walls since the thirteenth century, I don't believe it will ever fall out of fashion. Therefore, as it's a trend that is not going anywhere. This chapter is all about how to master the technique in your own home — the contemporary lines of shiplap, the grandeur of wainscot and those sharp Shaker styles — so that you're ready to start this super-satisfying DIY project. All the projects you see can be scaled up or down to suit your space and budget.

In this chapter I refer to MDF (Medium-density Fibreboard) as the preferred material for shiplap and Shaker-style panelling. It is relatively cheap and easily accessible. Pre-cut panelling packs are widely available, which you can simply buy and apply, but the most cost-effective way is to sketch your design and take your measurements to the in-house cutting service of your local DIY store, as then you have exactly what you need to fit your space and you avoid all the mess of cutting wood at home. I like to use 9mm- or 12mm-thick MDF for panelling as it creates impact without being too chunky and cumbersome. And for panelling in a bathroom or a kitchen, a moisture-resistant MDF is essential to ensure it doesn't swell or warp over time.

PANEL IT

MOULDING
Moulding, or what is sometimes referred to as 'wainscot moulding', is also an option when it comes to decorating a wall. Made from pine, these intricately shaped thin lengths are joined with mitred corners to create visually appealing boxes that add interest and depth to walls. Decorative lengths are available in many styles and thicknesses from the DIY store or you can buy ready-to-use packs if want to just take out the installation task, without the worry of measuring and cutting.

TONGUE AND GROOVE PANELS
Tongue and groove panels are thin, wider planks and are mostly made of spruce. Each panel features a tongue on one side which protrudes and slots into the groove of the next piece of panelling. Once fixed, the overall effect is of a larger uniformed pattern. Cut to fit a kitchen splashback, or built at full room height in a bootroom, the impact and versatility of tongue and groove mean this classic style is embraced in both period and contemporary interiors.

ACOUSTIC PANELS

Finally, trendy slatted 'acoustic panels' vary in quality but tend to be made from MDF strips that have been covered in a wood veneer, which are then stapled or glued to a thick foam backing. Incredibly versatile, these prefabricated panels can provide insulation and are ideal for hiding imperfect walls.

SHAKER-STYLE PANELLING

Shaker-style panelling was the first DIY project I ever posted on Instagram. I painted it in Farrow & Ball 'Railings' and couldn't get over the impact I'd achieved from my very reasonably priced sheet of MDF. It sparked my love for panelling and, since then, I have added every single style of panelling to my home. I hope this chapter will inspire you too.

In terms of installing panelling, there are two schools of thought. The 'quick and easy approach' applies a grab adhesive with the click of a cartridge gun and allows you time to wiggle, manoeuvre and straighten your panels while the glue dries. However, the issue with adhesive is that, if you change your mind or want to remove your panelling, you will also be removing chunks of plaster from the wall along with it. The slower, 'panel pin' technique is therefore recommended if you are concerned about this. Personally, I have used both techniques with great success.

HOW TO CREATE SHAKER-STYLE PANELLING

FULL DAY

The square lines and clean aesthetic of Shaker-style panelling mean it adapts effortlessly to many spaces in your home. Go for three-quarter height behind your bed, or half wall in a hallway, or make a statement with a full wall in a dining space. In essence, you are attaching MDF strips to a plastered wall, caulking the joins and painting it all in your colour of choice.

This specific project is for the impactful 'feature wall' at three-quarter height. It works wonderfully behind a bed or a sofa. For ease and speed, I will focus on the grab adhesive method in this guide. But whatever your DIY dream, the Shaker is gonna maker your wall! So let's measure up.

TROUBLESHOOTING

Before you start, think through the design as you need to decide on the spacing of the panels and the width of the battens. In most cases, spacing the panels 300-400mm apart works well, with battens that are 100mm wide. However, if you are unsure, take a photo of your wall and draw lines using the edit tool onto the photo. This instantly helps you to visualize the spacing and you'll be able to see how many styles look cool versus cluttered.

TOOLBOX

MDF strips –
  1350mm high x
  100mm wide x
  12mm thick
Grab adhesive
Spirit level
Panel pins or
  nail gun
Circular saw
  or hand saw
Caulk
Cartridge gun
Wood filler
180-grit
  sandpaper
Paintbrush
MDF primer
240-grit
  sandpaper
Topcoat paint
Paintbrush and
  mini roller

PANEL IT

Continues overleaf

1. First measure the height and width of your wall and decide how many panels you want to add to your wall. Remember that spacing between 300–400mm is the most aesthetically pleasing. As a guide, in my 3000mm-wide wall, I would choose to have eight battens.

2. You will also need the horizontal bars or 'rails' that sit at the top and bottom of the vertical posts. All you need is your wall width measurement, and multiply this by two.

See the box below for a simple formula for calculating what you need. My calculations for this project, appear in the worked example, right; you can adapt to suit your room.

3. Sketch out the design on paper and note if there are any plug sockets or light switches you will need to work around.

4. Take your measurements to the cutting desk at your local DIY store. Pick your preferred MDF sheet (9mm or 12mm thickness is recommended) and let them do the rest.

(Alternatively, you can buy a kit or, if you have the time, tools and confidence, bring the wood home to cut. But for ease here, let's assume the pieces have been cut to size.)

5. Now it's time to finalize the spacing of the vertical posts. This 3-step formula will help you calculate the spacing. I have given an example of how to use this formula, but replace with your own measurements. Mark the wall with pencil to indicate the position of the vertical posts.

Worked example:

A Number of battens (8) x width of battens (100mm) = 800mm

B Wall length (3000mm) – total width of all battens (800mm) = 2200mm

C 2200mm ÷ number of spaces (7) = spacing width (314mm)

6 Now it is time to install. First install the horizontal pieces that sit directly above the skirting board and run across the wall. Apply a thin bead of adhesive along the back of the MDF. Start near the corner, and run a zigzag pattern down the board. Lift and position it into the left side of the wall, pushing it so it sits flush on the top of the skirting board and meets the left corner of the wall. Check the alignment with a spirit level and apply firm pressure. Add the next horizontal piece and repeat until your first row is in place.

7 For the vertical pieces, start in the left corner. Apply the adhesive to the back as before and add it to the left corner so it sits flush on top of the horizontal rail and butts up to the corner of the wall. Check it is level using a spirit level – do not trust the corner of the wall alone as this may not be completely plumb!

8 Continue adding the vertical pieces along the wall, double checking the measurements and firmly pressing the panels to the wall. Grab adhesive has a drying time of up to 15 minutes, so there is time if you need to slightly readjust your pieces.

9 Once this is complete, take the remaining horizontal pieces and rest these on top of the verticals. Ensure they are level as this line will be at eye level. Add adhesive and apply pressure. Repeat until complete.

10 Optional extra – to finish off the top piece, a length of pine moulding can be added to aesthetically finish off the top of your panelling. Cut to size using a panel saw and secure with adhesive.

11 If you have older or irregular walls, you may need to hammer in a few 20mm panel pins. These are optional, but can secure the wood in place while it dries.

Continues overleaf

12 Apply wood filler to any joins/gaps visible between the MDF pieces. Leave to dry for an hour and sand until smooth with 180-grit sandpaper.

13 Apply decorator's caulk using a caulk gun to all the edges of MDF. Caulking the internal edges of the Shaker panels and along the top edge, and skirting will help achieve a professional result. Page 31 gives you the tips for perfect caulking!

14 Once the caulk has dried, choose an MDF primer and use a paintbrush to apply it to the wood. If you have chosen a dark-coloured topcoat, then a grey-tinted primer works best. If you are going with a light-coloured topcoat, then a white primer is perfect.

15 Once the primer has dried, have a look at the finish. Any bumps that catch your eye can be sanded back for a professional finish with a high-grit (minimum 240) paper.

16 Using a paintbrush to paint the internal corners between the panels, and a mini roller to fill in and paint the woodwork, apply the topcoat. Leave to dry. You will need 2–3 coats, depending on your emulsion.

17 Now step back and admire your work!

HOW TO CALCULATE YOUR SPACING

Use this formula to calculate your spacing.

```
number of battens (A) x width of battens (B) = C
wall length (D) - total width of all battens (C) = E
E ÷ number of spaces (A - 1) = spacing width (F)
```

HOW TO CREATE RECTANGULAR MOULDING

FULL DAY

Adding rectangular moulding to a wall can elevate the look of a room as it quietly provides additional texture and can help zone a space. The panelling style consists of mitred cornered boxes with a dado rail added above and for this project we will focus on mid-height moulding. However, if you want to adapt this project for full-wall impact, complete these steps and then add additional moulding boxes above the dado rail. Keep the same spacing but increase the vertical lengths of the rectangles.

Visually, rectangles approximately 700mm high x 530mm wide work well.

TROUBLESHOOTING:

- If you are inexperienced, buying a panel kit is recommended so you get perfectly measured and mitred cuts.
- Most DIY stores do not cut decorative mouldings down to size, so you can purchase lengths of pine moulding and use a mitre box and hand saw to make the cuts. If you have a circular or mitre power saw, it will make light work of these cuts. If you're up for the challenge, the guide to cutting wood can be found on page 70.

TOOLBOX

Pine moulding
Mitre box
Circular saw or hand saw
Pencil
Metal ruler
Spirit level
Grab adhesive
150-220-grit sandpaper
Cartridge gun
Caulk
Painter's tape
25mm brush
Wood primer
Topcoat paint
Foam roller

PANEL IT

Continues overleaf

1. As ever with panelling, nothing starts until you have measured up. See the box opposite for a simple formula for calculating what you need. Here are my calculations for this project:

Worked example:
Wall width spacing

A Rectangle width x 4:
530mm x 4 =
2120mm (B)

B Width of wall − B =
880mm (D)

C D ÷ 5 =
176mm (F)

2. Repeat the same formula to measure the vertical spacing. What is the desired height of your panelling? Subtract the length of your vertical pieces from the desired height.

For example:
1000mm−700mm= 300mm

You will need 2 x spaces top and bottom. Divide your calculated total by 2 to get the vertical spacing.

For example:
300mm ÷ 2 = 150mm

Worked example:
Wall height spacing

A Height of wall moulding −
rectangle height =
1000−700mm = 300mm (D)

B D ÷ 2 = 150mm (F)

3. If you have a ready-made kit, then skip this section! If you are cutting your own mitred corners, you will need to use your mitre box. Carefully make your cuts at a 45-degree angle using a fine-toothed saw.

4. Cut the length of dado rail to fit the width of your wall.

5. Using a pencil, metal ruler and spirit level, lightly draw your design onto the wall.

6. First up, add the dado rail, applying a thin bead of adhesive along the back, and using the pencil line as a guide, press it against the wall, working from left to right and using a spirit level to check it is level. Apply slow, firm pressure to the adhesive.

7. Now for the rectangles. Starting in the bottom left corner, fix a width of moulding to the wall along the bottom horizontal pencil line, using the same technique as your dado rail. Once the bottom rail is in place, add the two verticals and finally add the top horizontal bar. Check the mitred corners align and use a spirit level obsessively to check you are not wonky! Repeat until all the rectangles are in place.

8 Once the rectangles are all in position, wait until the adhesive (if using) has dried. If you have used panel pins, fill any holes with a little wood filler and, once it has dried, use a fine sanding paper (anything between 150–220 grit will be fine) to achieve a smooth surface.

9 Using a cartridge gun (see page 15), caulk all the edges of the dado rail and moulding. There is the saying that 'we try our best and caulk the rest' so, if you have any small imperfections, the caulk should smooth over them to create a seamless finish.

10 Once the caulk has dried, you're ready to paint. Run painter's tape all along the top edge of the dado rail to ensure you achieve a crisp line (see page 134), then, using a 25mm brush, paint the wood moulding with wood primer. Leave to dry.

11 Paint the mouldings and wall with emulsion paint in your chosen colour to create a seamless finish. Paint the edges of the wood first with a brush, before using a short- to mid-pile roller to fill in the rest of the wall.

HOW TO CALCULATE YOUR MOULDINGS

Use this formula to calculate your spacing and also need to work out how many panels you can fit in the available space?

rectangle width/height (A) x number of rectangles = B
wall width/moulding height (C) - B = D
D ÷ number of spaces (B + 1)= Spacing width (F)

HOW TO INSTALL ACOUSTIC PANELLING

FULL DAY

Acoustic panelling is a modern style of panelling that uses slim, prefabricated MDF panels, wrapped in a wood veneer and with a thick foam backing. The latter absorbs sound, so this panelling works well in areas of the home which are heavily tiled (the kitchen, for example) or those heavy-traffic areas. It is also ideal for helping to conceal damaged walls and can be used to make 'hidden' doors as the closely positioned slats can easily be cut and joined to create a seamless look across a wall. The foam has insulating qualities and can cosy up a space with its natural wood grain texture and colour. It is available in wood shades from light ash through to the deepest walnut and so can suit almost every interior. The prefab panels are easy to cut and secure, so modify this tutorial to suit your wall height.

TOOLBOX

Acoustic panels
Masking tape
Pencil
Stanley knife
Circular saw or hand saw
Fine-grit sandpaper
Drill
Jigsaw to cut around sockets
Grab adhesive
3mm drill bit
Screws and wall plugs

TROUBLESHOOTING

- Always add an extra 10 per cent to your order to allow for wastage and, let's face it, human error. It happens!
- If your walls are uneven or if you're concerned about removing the panels at a later date, I'd recommend screwing the panels into the wall for peace of mind and less damage than bonding to the wall with adhesive.

This guide is for full-height wall installation. The feature wall is back!

1. Measure the height and width of your wall. Acoustic panels are largely available in 2400mm or 3000mm lengths and are typically 600mm wide. Divide your wall width by 600mm to calculate how many panels you will need to purchase. For example, if my wall is 3.6m wide by 2.35m high, I will need to purchase 6 x 240cm panels.

2. Acoustic panels can be cut to size by layering masking tape to the top of the wooden slats and drawing your pencil line onto the tape. Score or indent this line using a Stanley knife to leave a guide for the cut. The tape will reduce the chance of splintering the wood.

3. Using a fine-toothed saw, cut horizontally along the slats. Ask someone to hold the panel for you or clamp the panel to a table while making this cut. Lightly sand the newly cut ends if needed using a fine sandpaper grit (see page 29).

4. If you have to cut the remaining piece down to size to fit, use a Stanley knife to cut through the felt backing.

5. If you have switches or sockets to navigate, align your wall panel to the socket. Mark onto your panel the section that needs removing. Drill a hole through the centre of this mark and use a jigsaw to remove the unwanted square of panelling.

6. To secure to the wall with adhesive, apply grab adhesive along the back of the panel in a zigzag line from top to bottom. Lift the first panel and press into the left corner of your wall. Check with a spirit level and then push firmly at the top, middle and bottom of the panel, maintaining pressure for several minutes for the adhesive to start to cure. Repeat with each panel, moving from left to right across the wall until your feature wall is complete.

7. To secure with screws and wall plugs, lift your panel up to the wall and ask a partner to hold it in its intended position. Drill three holes through the black felt backing at the top, middle and bottom of your panel with a 3mm multi-use drill bit. Let the drill mark the wall as it exits the felt backing. This will be your guide when drilling into the wall.

   It is recommended to use 12–15 35mm x 3.5mm screws per panel. So repeat this until all holes have been made.

8. Lift the panel off and using the markings as your guide, drill into the wall with 3.5mm masonry drill bit and insert 3.5mm wall plugs into these holes. Line your acoustic panel back up and screw in through the black felt until the screw anchors into the wall plug.

HOW TO CREATE TONGUE AND GROOVE PANELLING

FULL DAY

Tongue and groove (T&G) panelling evokes a timeless style, synonymous with cottages and a more traditional period style of home. However, there are no rules when it comes to panelling, and the vertical lines of T&G now adorn hallways, kitchens and bathrooms, at mid- and full-height, in homes and of every style and description. T&G, often made from spruce, is available in packs of planks or as prefabricated panels that contain the grooved detail, which are wider and pre-primed. This can save time and labour but they are more expensive. For this project, I've used unprimed, spruce T&G planks, and the panelled look will be achieved by slotting the protruding 'tongue' on one edge into the 'groove' of the next plank. The top edge can be finished off with the addition of moulding — square-cut moulding gives a more contemporary and clean finish, however for this project I will choose to add a more decorative pine moulding for a traditional look. This project uses pre-cut planks that are 1800mm high, to create a panelled area featuring coat hooks in an entrance hall.

TROUBLESHOOTING

- Check the panels before you buy to ensure the grooves are not damaged and that there is no sign of warping.
- For homes with wonky walls, you may need to hammer in panel pins or use a nail gun to hold the planks in place.
- If you have any obstacles to contend with, such as sockets or switches, measure their position onto your panel and use a jigsaw to cut them out (see page 74).
- If you get to the end of the wall and have an awkward measurement to deal with, cut the final panel to size with a hand saw or circular saw. Whether you are using a manual or power tool, be sure to clamp the wood to your worktable before you start and sanding the cut edge.

TOOLBOX

```
1800mm pine T&G
  planks
Hand saw or
  circular saw,
  if using
Ruler
Spirit level
Pencil
Cartridge gun
Grab adhesive
25mm panel pins
  or nail gun
Knotting solution
Decorator's caulk
Wood filler
180-grit
  sandpaper
Painter's tape
Wood primer
Topcoat paint
50mm paintbrush
100mm mini foam
  roller
```

1. Measure the width of the wall to calculate the number of planks you require.

   Worked example:
   Wall width 2000mm
   Plank width 95mm

   2000 ÷ 95 = 21.05
   (at this stage I would choose to have 21 planks, and add caulk to fill any gap left)

2. Using a ruler and a spirit level, lightly pencil a horizontal line onto the wall to mark the height of the panelling.

3. Securing the first panel is critical. Beginning in the left corner of the wall, use a spirit level to find the plumb line. With a cartridge gun, apply a thin bead of grab adhesive in a diagonal line down the plank, zigzagging your way from top to bottom, then align it with the plumb line to ensure it is completely straight, with the lip (tongue) out ready to receive the next panel, and secure it into place by pressing it firmly to the wall. There may be an awkward gap between the plank and the wall, but we can fill that at the end!

4. Working left to right, keep applying adhesive and slotting the planks into place. The tongues and grooves should fit together like a jigsaw.

5. Now it's time to trim the top edge of the panelling with your chosen moulding. Secure it across the top of the T&G panels with adhesive and leave to dry.

6. Apply knotting solution to the pine knots. There is normally a small brush provided in the lid of this product. This may seem tedious but it will prevent the sap from the pine knots eventually leaking through the paint. Leave to dry.

7. Caulk the top edge of the moulding and any spaces between the planks and the wall. Leave to dry.

8. Apply painter's tape along the top edge of the moulding to ensure you achieve crisp lines. With a 50mm brush, apply one coat of wood primer to the panelling, working it into the grooves, then leave to dry.

9. With a 50mm paintbrush, paint in the grooves and cut in the top of the panelling. Using a small foam roller, paint the remainder of each plank in a vertical motion. This will need two coats.

10. To make this space functional, add coat hooks at intervals along the width of the panelling.

ALTERNATIVE METHOD

Mid-height T&G panels (900mm and 1200mm) work well for many spaces in the home. Coat hooks, however, need a little extra height (1800mm lengths). If you require a custom height for a project, you can cut the panels to size using a panel saw or circular saw.

> **TOP TIP**
> Check you can reach the hook height! Consider adding a couple of hooks lower down for children so they can reach too.

HOW TO SHIPLAP A WALL

Shiplap offers a more contemporary, clean-line aesthetic than the traditional tongue and groove panelling. Made from thin strips of MDF, it is also relatively inexpensive compared to other forms of panelling. It can be laid vertically or horizontally and is a great solution to conceal uneven walls. If you are installing them vertically, follow the same principle as the tongue and groove panelling guide above, working from left to right and using a spirit level to ensure the first panel is plumb. However, in my opinion, shiplap looks fantastic when installed horizontally, with a 2mm tile spacer to create a shadow gap between the planks, so we'll focus on this method here. Here's how to add horizontal shiplap to a full wall.

TOOLBOX

MDF planks
Cartridge gun
Grab adhesive
Laser or spirit level
Panel pins or nail gun
Hammer
Tile spacers (2mm)
Spirit level
Circular saw or hand saw
Wood filler
180-grit sandpaper
Decorator's caulk
Paintbrush
Wood primer
Topcoat paint
Mini roller, if using

TROUBLESHOOTING

- To get the best finish, we will be installing horizontal shiplap from the top down. If working at height, ensure you have a second person to support the ladder and assist in lifting the panels.
- The panels will be fighting gravity. Ensure you have fully secured each panel to the wall using the grab adhesive and panel pins, before moving on to the next.
- Follow the line of the spirit or laser level, not your walls. Small discrepancies with wonky walls can be visually corrected with caulk after.

1. Measure the wall you wish to panel and calculate how many planks you will need for your space. Here is my worked example:

   Shiplap plank is 180mm wide
   Wall height is 2400mm
   2400 ÷ 180 = 13.3 planks

   However, the 2mm gaps between panels will adjust the number of planks you will need, and you may end up having to cut a length to fit, or there is a little hack you can try to conceal the corner with no cutting needed!

2. We will start at the top when laying horizontally, as this first plank will be highly visible and therefore needs to be a full plank. Start in the top left-hand corner. With a cartridge gun, apply a thin bead of grab adhesive in a diagonal line down the plank, zigzagging your way from top to bottom. Using a spirit level to ensure it is completely straight, secure it into place by pressing it firmly into the wall.

   There may be an awkward gap between the plank and the ceiling, but we can fill that at the end! Fixing 30mm panel pins at 600mm intervals with a hammer will provide additional support and stop it from sliding.

3. Now you are ready for your next plank so get ready with your adhesive and 2mm tile spacers that will give you that desirable shadow gap. Apply a thin bead of adhesive to the plank and position it on the wall using a spirit level for alignment. Slot 2mm tile spacers between the planks at approximately 300mm intervals. Hammer in panel pins again at 60mm intervals to hold this piece in place.

4. Keep repeating steps 2 and 3 as you work down the wall and keep checking with a spirit level to ensure your lines are keeping straight.

5. When you reach the bottom, you can either cut a final piece to size with a circular saw or hand saw, or fill the space with smaller offcuts of MDF. Alternatively, using a thinner 3mm plank of MDF, position the final plank so it sits flush with the skirting board. This will conceal any awkward gaps that have been left.

6. Fill your pin holes with wood filler and, once dried, sand back with 180-grit sandpaper.

7. Using a cartridge gun, caulk the outer edges where they meet adjoining walls/skirting board/ceiling of the panels and leave to dry.

8. With a brush, paint the MDF with wood primer and leave to dry.

9. Using a large brush, paint the wall with two coats of your topcoat paint. If you did paint the inner joins, this final topcoat can be completed with a mini roller.

HOW TO PANEL UP THE STAIRS

If you've had a go at some panelling and feel ready for the next challenge, it's time for you to master the advanced art of staircase angles and corners. For this project, your best friend will be an angle finder measuring tool — do buy one if you don't have one already. They can be mechanical or digital but are guaranteed to speed up the measuring and planning process and improve your accuracy.

TROUBLESHOOTING

If you find the angles confusing, there are numerous apps and websites that can calculate your cuts for you. Search for 'mitre angle calculator' to get some extra reassurance.

TOOLBOX
Dado rail
Pine moulding
Tape measure
Pencil
Angle finder
Mitre saw
100mm wooden offcut block
Grab adhesive
Panel pins or nail gun
Hand saw
Mitre box or shears
Caulk
Cartridge gun
Wood filler
120-grit sandpaper
Wood primer
Topcoat paint

PANEL IT

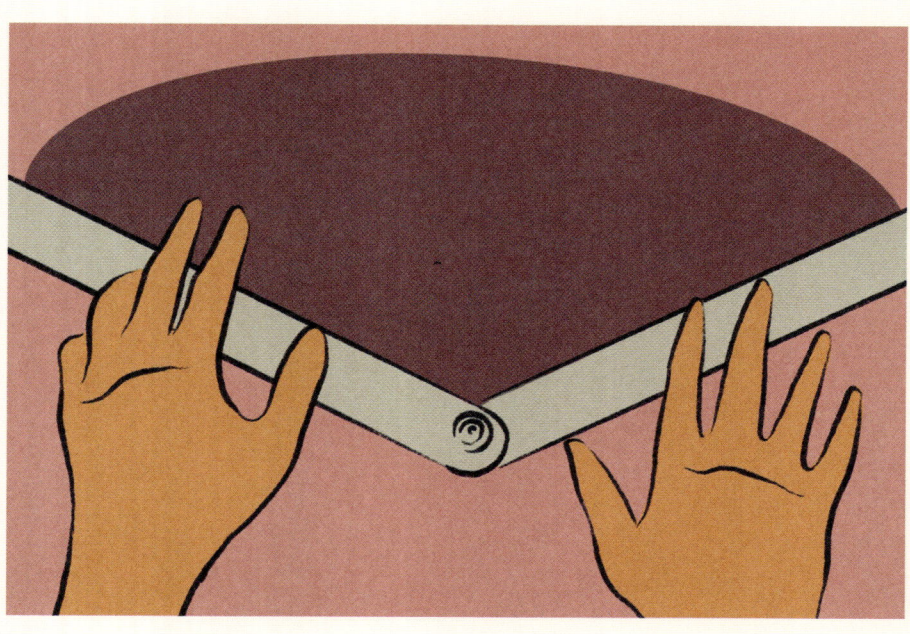

1. First create the dado rail. Start with the flat areas, such as the stair landing. Measure 1m in a straight vertical line from the skirting board and draw a horizontal pencil line across the wall. Check with a spirit level. The dado rail will sit on this line.

2. Now work down/up the stairs: measure 1m in a straight vertical line from the skirting board and mark the wall accordingly. Connect the pencil marks with a straight, angled line. The dado rail will sit on this line.

3. Using an angle finder, measure the angles of your pencil lines and halve this angle to find your cutting angle.

   For example: if the angle where the dado rail on the stairs meets the landing is 140 degrees, as shown below, halve this to find your cutting angle: 70 degrees.

4. Measure the length of the dado rail pieces and cut the angles using a mitre saw.

5. Now onto the inner panels. Use a 100mm wood offcut to measure even spacing at the top under the dado rail and bottom above the skirting board and mark these points with a pencil line.

6. The points where the pencil lines crossover between the angled dado rail and the flat landing sections determine where your moulding boxes will start and finish. Draw these vertical lines onto the wall.

Continues overleaf

PANEL IT

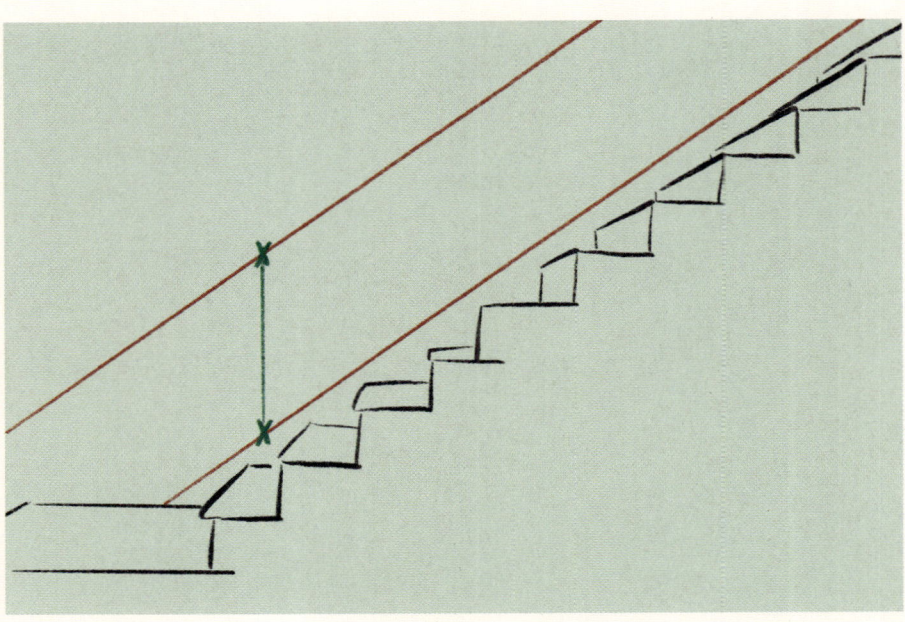

183

7 Measure the length between the two vertical lines you have just drawn to calculate how many panels you wish to install.

Worked example:
If the distance is 3200mm and you wish to install four panels, you will have 3 x 100mm gaps that need to be deducted.
3200−300 = 2900mm
2900mm ÷ 4 panels = 725mm in panel width

8 Draw the panel templates onto the wall, using your 100mm offcut to ensure the spacing between the verticals is even.

9 Now measure the angles for cutting the moulding.
To measure the obtuse angle, use your angle finder ÷ 2
To measure the acute angle:
180 minus the obtuse measurement ÷ 2
To check you are correct the total of all four angles will total 360 degrees.

When working along the landing, or flat areas, horizontal lengths will be cut at 45-degree angles to make a right angle. You can cut these angles with a hand saw on a mitre box, or use mitre shears if your moulding is thin.

As with all panelling projects, the wood will need filling, caulking around the joins where it meets the wall, priming and painting. You can find more detail here:

- Wood filler is used to fill any gaps at the mitred corners, apply with your finger, leave to dry and use fine-grit sandpaper to smooth over (see page 29).

- Caulk is applied to create a smooth join on the inside and outside edges where the moulding meets the wall. It is paintable and creates a professional-looking finish (see page 31).

- Wood primer seals the wood and blocks stains. It provides the perfect surface for your topcoat.

- Paint your stair panelling in the same paint as your wall — a scrubbable paint is recommended (see page 120).

ALTERNATIVE METHOD

Now, let's be frank! That is a lot of maths and a lot of calculating. However, as with any DIY, there is always an optional shortcut. Using cardboard to make a template of your moulding, mark the angles onto your wall as before, then replicate this onto cardboard. Cut this shape out and then cut it in half from the corners. This gives you a template of your cut line. Clamping this onto your moulding, make your mitre cut in line with the cardboard. This will give you a 'good enough' result which can be improved with filler and caulk.

In many countries around the world, the number of people renting their homes is on the rise. This trend is being driven by many factors, like rising housing costs, economic instability and demographic changes. However, many people, especially in cities, also choose to rent their homes as it provides greater flexibility in relation to changes in situation, such as with work and relationships.

Depending on tenancy rules, rental homes can come with decor limitations, especially with regard to drilling and permanently fixing into the walls or switching up the fixtures and fittings. Many landlords are relaxed about such things as a happy tenant is more likely to look after their property, but I recommend checking with them or your lettings agency before you add a shelf for storage or a blackout blind to improve your sleep.

Even if there are strict rules to your tenancy agreement, there are still so many ways for you to add character and personality to your rental space through DIY and styling. The evolution of removable wallpapers, vinyl and damage-free fixings means that spaces can be transformed and then returned to their original condition with ease. In fact, searching for 'rental decor' and 'renter hacks' on social media will uncover more inspiration than you will know what to do with. So, hang your art. Swap the curtains. Wrap that kitchen and put your own stamp on your home, for however long or short your lease. Let's unlock that Positive Rental Attitude!

RENT IT

HOW TO WRAP KITCHEN COUNTER TOPS

If you inherit a kitchen you dislike, there are many ways to deal with it. Changing the handles over or adding 'peel and stick' tiles to the splashback can update the vibe and bring in your own personality. The worktop can also be transformed with vinyl roll. Wood effect, terrazzo or even marbled designs can refresh the space in a day. But better still, it can also be removed! Both deposit-friendly and cost-effective — winning!

TOOLBOX

Silicone removal tool
Stanley knife
Sugar soap
Tape measure
Pencil
Vinyl roll
Scissors
Squeegee
Seam roller to seal the edges
Hair dryer
Acetone or adhesive cleaner (for removal)

TROUBLESHOOTING

- You may need to remove the hob or the sink if these sit flush with the worktop area.
- If you do not have a squeegee, a credit card, library card or 'whoops I forgot to return it' hotel door card will also do the same job.
- If noticeable folds or bumps appear in the vinyl, peel the section back and reapply. If your vinyl overstretches or puckers, you may need to replace the piece and start again.

RENT IT

1. Prepare the surface by removing the existing silicone from the edges of the worktop. Use a silicone removal tool, or if you're very careful, a Stanley knife. Take care to cut and peel it off without damaging the existing worktop.

2. Using sugar soap, clean the surface to remove all traces of grease and grime, to ensure it is smooth and clear.

3. Measure up the sections of worktop you wish to cover. You may wish to sketch a plan so you can easily and quickly refer to these measurements. Allow 100mm excess for wrapping the vinyl over the edges of the worktops, which will later be trimmed away underneath.

4. Transfer your measurements onto the vinyl roll and, using sharp scissors or a Stanley knife, cut your first section to size. Re-measure and cut each section as you go — do not cut them all out at the start, in case you need to adjust.

5. Roll out the first section of vinyl. In the top-left corner, peel off a small amount of the backing paper and position it in the top-left corner of your worktop section, lining it up with wall. If your corner is not flush with a wall, leave 100mm of excess to cover the edge.

6. Gently and slowly smooth the vinyl down, from the centre towards the edges. If you see air bubbles appear, use a squeegee (normally provided with the vinyl), to push out the air bubbles. Work the squeegee up and down and from left to right, with no gaps between the squeegee lines. This will reduce the chances of air gaps forming.

7. To manoeuvre the vinyl over the edges use a hair dryer to gently warm the material. This makes it more pliable and easier to fold over the edge.

8. Using a sharp knife (snap a new blade if you can), cut your material at the edges so it sits flush against any walls, and trim away the excess. Smooth the edges down to seal them and ensure thorough adhesion of the vinyl.

9. If you find a bubble after sealing your edges, apply a little heat with a hair dryer as this may be enough for it to disperse with a small push from a squeegee. If not, prick the smallest of holes in the bubble with a needle and gently press the vinyl back down.

10. When it's time to remove vinyl wrap, heat with a hair dryer, starting at the edges and moving to the centre, and slowly pull the vinyl back on itself at an angle (not upwards). Remove any adhesive using acetone or an adhesive cleaner.

HOW TO INSTALL 'PEEL AND STICK' WALLPAPER

FULL DAY

'Peel and stick' wallpaper can add colour and pattern to a wall without the mess or long-term commitment of wallpapering, which makes it perfect for renters or indecisive decorators who want to test out interior vibes! It is sold by the roll, for you to cut and fit to your specific space, or you can purchase a made-to-measure mural from a website. One of my favourite decor hacks is to create a bespoke wallpaper from vinyl wall stickers. Particularly in children's rooms, where tastes and interests can evolve, removing vinyl dinosaurs and replacing it with footballs can be an inexpensive way to keep a space fresh and fun. This guide focuses on installing 'peel and stick' wallpaper by the roll, but you can follow the same preparation steps for applying wall stickers or larger vinyl colour blocks too.

TOOLBOX
Cloth
180-grit sandpaper, if using 'Peel and stick' mural/wallpaper
Measuring tape
Sharp scissors
Pencil
Spirit level
Squeegee
Seam roller
Wallpaper knife
Hairdryer
Tweezers

TROUBLESHOOTING

- Bumpy walls are a potential problem as indents and protrusions can show through your wallpaper. If you are looking to conceal a damaged wall with peel and stick wallpaper, choose a busy pattern that will distract the eye from focusing on any imperfections.
- Another potential issue can arise with air bubbles being trapped. Work slowly and smooth out to the edges to reduce these occurring.

RENT IT

1. Dust the wall down thoroughly as the wallpaper will adhere best to a clean and dry surface. If you can, smooth away any wall imperfections as this will enhance the finish. If renting, you may not wish to use sandpaper on your walls, but a light rub by hand with 180-grit paper would smooth out any imperfections.

2. Measure the height of the wall and cut the first length of paper with sharp scissors, leaving an overhang of 50mm at the top and bottom of the wall.

3. Measure the width of your wallpaper and transfer this measurement across onto the wall. Draw a plumb line onto the wall using a spirit level and pencil — this will determine the edge of your first piece.

4 From the top of your first drop, peel off 200mm of backing paper, then hold the paper up to your wall, ensuring there is overhang at the ceiling/top and at the bottom (the excess can be trimmed later).

5 Align the paper to the plumb line, check its positioning again, then stick it to the wall, pushing and smoothing the paper flat with a squeegee tool, or if you do not have one, use your hands. If you are worried about alignment at this point, you have a small window to adjust the paper before it adheres fully to the wall, but act fast!

6 Gently peel off the paper backing as you smooth the vinyl onto the wall, working from top to bottom. Smooth down with a squeegee tool and push any air bubbles or creases out to the edges.

7 Now line up the next section. If your wallpaper is patterned, take good care to ensure that the pattern matches the first drop. As you position the second piece, overlap the first drop by 2mm. Vinyl wallpapers will experience more shrinkage than traditional paper, so this gentle overlap will reduce the chances of wall lines appearing between sheets.

8 Use a seam roller or any smoothing tool to flatten any visible edges and continue to work from left to right, applying gentle pressure to the wallpaper. Vinyl can stretch and pucker if it is overworked, so handle with care. Keep adding sections, remembering to overlap the preceding drop each time by 2mm, until you have papered the entire wall.

9 When you have finished hanging the paper, it's time to trim the edges. Using a wallpaper knife, cut along the skirting board and ceiling line to create a clean edge. If you feel any drag or resistance when cutting, your blade is blunt, so snap a new blade to avoid tears.

10 If your tenancy is up or you just fancy a refresh, removing 'peel and stick' wallpaper is easy, but not quick! Starting in the top-left corner, use a hairdryer on a low setting to warm the paper and soften the adhesive. Resist the urge to yank the vinyl! Just add heat, gently prise the paper from the wall and it should slowly peel off. If there is any sticky residue, warm water and washing-up liquid applied with a cloth can be used to gently wipe it off. Alternatively, use a hairdryer on the sticky areas, and prise off the residue with tweezers.

TOP TIP

When removing the wallpaper, if there is any resistance, continue to apply heat until it loosens. Pulling it too quickly can remove paint or even damage the plaster, so take your time.

HOW TO HANG PICTURE FRAMES WITH NO SCREWS

A gallery wall is still possible even if you do not want to mark your walls, thanks to the invention of Velcro hanging strips. These use Velcro technology to lock together two adhesive parts, which adhere to a wall and to the back of a frame and, if applied correctly, can provide a secure fix for lightweight frames. I say can, because there are always going to be factors that affect the adhesion, so please read the safety note below. However, in my experience, they are great for hanging lightweight frames and so are perfect for renters or, if like me, you have a constant itch to keep changing and adding to your art collection. They can be used on metal, tiled walls, painted plaster and glass, so they are incredibly versatile.

TOOLBOX
Cloth
Tape measure
Pencil
Velcro strips
Spirit level

TROUBLESHOOTING
This method is not recommended for use in children's rooms, or above beds, or in spaces with hard tiled flooring, which could be damaged by a falling frame!

1. Clean the wall to remove any dust that could affect the adhesion. Ensure the wall is completely dry before you start. If you have a freshly painted wall, leave this to cure for at least 7 days before using these strips.

2. Measure out where you would like your frames to go using a tape measure. If needed, lightly mark the wall with a pencil. Bear in mind, if you move out, you will need to clean any pencil marks off the walls!

3. Align two Velcro strips and click them together to bond the two pieces.

4. Remove the protective paper from one strip and stick it to the back edge of the picture frame. Positioning it roughly 2mm from the edge of the frame will ensure it cannot be seen from the front.

5. Remove the protective paper from the wall-side strip and stick your frame to the wall, ensuring it is straight by using a spirit level. Press each corner firmly for at least 30 seconds.

6. Tilt the bottom of the frame away from the wall so that the Velcro unlocks, leaving the wall-side strip in position on the wall. Press each corner firmly into the wall again.

7. Leave the strip to cure into the wall for 1 hour before reattaching your frame. When you do, you will hear the frame 'click' into place.

8. To remove your frames, tilt the bottom away from the wall — do not pull them straight off. If you need to remove the strip, use one hand to hold the strip against the wall and the other hand to pull the removal strip downwards, slowly. Keep it slow and smooth to ensure you do not remove any paint from your walls.

RENT IT

USEFUL HACKS FOR INSTALLING 'NO-DAMAGE' LIGHTING

In many homes the lighting we acquire is limited to a big central ceiling light or a smattering of LED spotlights. When renting, it is unlikely that a landlord will accommodate any requests for aesthetic lighting but worry not, as we can bring the vibes DIY-style and, best of all, remove them so they can be packed up and reinstalled somewhere else in the future.

Rechargeable battery lights have revolutionized lighting options for our homes. Table lamps are no longer tethered to the wall and wall lights do not require expensive electrical wiring and all the upheaval that can bring to our home. Here are five of the best to try in your space.

STRIP LIGHTS
USB-charged strip lights can be used to bring a subtle but interesting light effect. Position them on or underneath shelving, around a mirror or behind furniture. Illuminating features of your home that you love draws attention to them and can also distract from the areas you want to hide!

PENDANT LIGHTS
Lightweight shades can be hung with any cord or cable of your choosing and attached to the ceiling using an adhesive hook. Secure a battery-operated puck light (a small, LED light that is shaped like a puck) inside the shade and use the remote control to operate the light.

WALL LIGHTS
Self-adhesive wall sconces can be combined with rechargeable bulbs for a damage-free lighting solution. Alternatively, plug-in wall lights can work, but will require two small screws to secure the wall fixing. On removal, fill the hole in the plaster (see page 44) and touch up the paint. I know this is titled 'no damage' but, if removed correctly, no one will ever know!

STRING LIGHTS
Festoon or fairy lights instantly make a home feel cosy, so who said they are only for Christmas or pergolas? Drape them across your space, however you like, and use self-adhesive hooks to secure them in place. This works well for both battery- and mains-operated lights, and they can easily be moved around your home to freshen up the décor when it's feeling a bit tired.

UNLOCK YOUR P.R.A.

(POSITIVE RENTAL ATTITUDE)

Upcycling has risen in popularity in recent years and is a great way to reduce waste and adapt to the ever-changing trends and inspirations delivered to us via social media. Instead of replacing items of furniture and accessories, rejuvenating them saves us all a lot of money, plus it's fun to look at the existing pieces in our homes, to get creative and to give them a new lease of life. This way, our interiors keep feeling fresh and exciting, plus we reduce the amount of landfill and the environmental impact of furniture production.

The quality and longevity of old pieces of furniture are now often in stark contrast to the quality and durability of contemporary pieces, which are often made cheaply with particle-board construction. In fact, there really is no comparison. However, charity shops are full of old, good-quality items and, by restoring and fixing these classic pieces, we not only do something good for the planet but we also bring a little bit of character and history into our homes. Sprucing up a preloved piece with a lick of paint costs a small fraction of what you would spend to buy new, so it's no wonder that, according to the online retailer Missoma, 25–34-year-olds are most likely to upcycle or recycle furniture.

The Covid-19 lockdowns also had an impact on home upcycling. Suddenly, confined to our homes and with plenty of time to spare, we began to unleash our creative abilities and address the niggles we'd always had with the things around us. I, for one, found myself adorning an old IKEA HEMNES chest of drawers with 1,000 wooden lollipop sticks and a tube of No More Nails. And it was the first time a social media post of mine ever went viral, plus it helped pass a few hours, so win-win!

The techniques in this chapter can be applied to thrifted items or those with unlocked potential within your home. Saving furniture from landfill is our mission, and the possibilities are endless…

UPCYCLE IT

HOW TO UPCYCLE A VASE WITH BICARB-TEXTURED PAINT

QUICK & QUIET

Minimalist home decor replaces colour with texture, layering neutrals and organic shapes. This interiors trend continues to dominate homeware stores and Pinterest boards, and can even be created at home with just a quick visit to the kitchen cupboard for some bicarbonate of soda, which will give you that boho chic aesthetic for free. Preloved vases, glasses, candle sticks and ornaments can all be made over and, once you've tried this creative hack, nothing will be safe!

TOOLBOX

```
Table protection
Microfibre cloth
Paint mixing bowl
250ml/1 cup paint
  (acrylic/
  emulsion/
  latex-based)
1 tablespoon
  bicarbonate of
  soda (baking
  soda)
Small paintbrush
```

TROUBLESHOOTING

```
Build up thin layers of paint, rather than going for
one thick layer, as this means the paint will adhere
better to the vase.
```

1. Clean your chosen vase and remove any dust or grime as this will improve the bond between the textured paint mixture and the surface. Dry thoroughly with a microfibre cloth.

2. Create a raised shelf on your worktop where you can sit the vase, so you are able to paint as many sides/angles as possible without having to touch it.

3. In a mixing bowl, combine the paint and bicarbomate of soda to create a thick, textured paste. If you are not ready to use it straight away, cover the bowl with clingfilm as the mixture dries very quickly.

4. Using a small paintbrush, sweep the textured paste across the vase. Build up thinner layers, rather than going for one thick layer as this means the paint will adhere better to the vase. Leave to dry between layers.

5. Add another layer of paint, this time creating more texture by stippling (using the ends of the paint bristles to apply the paint). Leave to dry for 15 minutes. Add more textured paint layers until you are happy with the result (personal preference!). Stand back and admire your textured clay-like ornament and do a happy dance to celebrate all the money you have saved!

HOW TO CREATE OAK CEILING BEAMS

1+ DAYS

(DEPENDENT ON THE AREA YOU'RE PAINTING)

Dark-painted ceiling beams and furniture can make a room feel dark and smaller as the ceiling height feels lower. Cosy to some, but oppressive to others. Of course, you can spend time and money sandblasting beams and stripping back layers of old paint. However, why bother when you can use this clever paint combination to lighten dark beams to look like warm, honeyed 'oak'? In fact, a creative day with a paintbrush can do the trick! This project below refers to painting ceiling beams, but you can apply the same methods to many other parts of the home, like a fireplace mantel or stair banister.

TROUBLESHOOTING

- Ensure your floor and furniture are protected as painting ceilings is always messy work.
- There are many paints that require no primer and are 'self-levelling' – these paints provide a durable and flat finish ready for the browning wax.
- Neutral paint colours such as Frenchic's Crème de la Crème, or Dulux Classic Cream will work.

TOOLBOX

Hoover or handheld brush
50mm paintbrush
Neutral-coloured, self-priming, water-based paint
Stiff bristle brush or waxing brush
Browning wax
Lint-free buffing cloth

1 Using a hoover-attachment brush or a handheld brush, dust the beams to remove any loose particles that can affect the paint adhesion.

2 Using a 50mm paintbrush, coat the beams in the neutral-coloured paint. At this point, you are going to get the 'first-coat paint fear' but be brave and persevere as you will add the depth and tone in the next step. Assess if you need a second coat of paint by looking at the coverage. If the dark beam colour is still visible, then you will need to give the beams a second coat. If you are happy, then leave to fully dry for 4 hours. If you attempt to wax sooner than this, you may brush off the lighter base coat.

3 Load a stiff bristle brush or waxing brush with browning wax and apply to the beams, using a circular motion at first, then work the wax into the wood with short strokes. Leave the wax for 15 minutes to penetrate the wood before adding more.

4 Apply the wax liberally and keep layering the colour until you achieve your desired 'wood tone'. If you wish to remove some of the product, use a lint-free buffing cloth, which will lighten the tone.

ALTERNATIVE METHOD

If your beams look too 'new' and planed, you can add texture to give them more of an aged, rustic look. Using a hammer and chisel, gently 'rough up' the surface of the beams on all sides as this variation in texture will complement the variation in colour.

HOW TO MAKEOVER PINE FURNITURE SCANDI-STYLE

Upcycling doesn't need to involve a drastic change or even require a lot of work. With a little white wax, you can neutralize the 'orange' tone of pine furniture to give it a more contemporary Scandi-style look. The extra advantages are that you retain the warmth, texture and grain of natural wood and also provide it with a protective and durable top layer.

TROUBLESHOOTING
White wax (or liming wax, to use its alternative name) can be added on top of varnished or oiled surfaces, but sanding will improve the adhesion of the wax.

TOOLBOX
Medium-grit and fine-grit sandpaper
Cloth
Stiff bristle brush
White wax (liming wax)
Lint-free buffing cloth

1 First sand the wood with a medium-grit paper, before working up to a fine-grit to achieve a smooth finish. Remove the dust and clean with a damp cloth, then leave to dry.

2 Using a waxing brush, liberally apply the white wax onto the wood and use a lint-free buffing cloth to rub the wax into the grain. The tone of the wood will lighten for a more contemporary finish.

3 Leave the item overnight to dry completely.

HOW TO CREATE A CHECKERBOARD CHEST OF DRAWERS

QUICK & QUIET

Upcycling furniture doesn't simply have to mean a fresh coat of paint as, with the help of a little masking tape/painter's tape, you can experiment with all kinds of striped, checkered and abstract designs. One of my favourite pieces at home is a pine chest of drawers which was a very uninspiring piece, before I used masking tape to create a vertical checkerboard effect on the drawer fronts.

TROUBLESHOOTING

- To maximize efficiency on your 'DIY Do-Day', plan your design out beforehand. Sketch your ideas on a piece of paper or take a photo of your furniture and play around using the 'mark-up' tool on your phone to draw directly onto the photo. Once you are happy, you are ready to go.
- If adding stripes or a checkerboard design, an odd number will allow you to have a centrally positioned shape, whereas if you go even, your design will split in the middle of your furniture, leaving alternate colours at each end of the drawer front.
- As with all upcycles, the result is determined by the prep. If your furniture has existing varnish or paint, strip it back to expose the raw wood (see page 34 to recap all your stripping options).
- Eggshell or satin paint works beautifully on wood, but if you prefer a matt look try a chalk paint. Emulsion is not recommended on furniture due to the likelihood of it chipping.
- Many brands sell a 'delicate surfaces' version of their masking tape which has less adhesive and is therefore less likely (but not guaranteed) to remove the base paint when you remove the tape.

TOOLBOX

120-grit and 220-grit sandpaper
Cloth
Small foam roller
Wood primer
2 x contrasting eggshell paints
Mini roller paint tray
25mm angled paintbrush
Ruler
Pencil
Laser level
Masking tape
Mini foam roller
Furniture finishing wax and waxing brush, if using

Continues overleaf

1. Remove the drawers, unscrew any knobs or handles and sand the chest of drawers first with a medium-grit sandpaper, before working up to a fine-grit paper to smooth and perfect the finish. Remember to work in the direction of the grain. Clean with a damp cloth and leave to dry.

2. Using a small foam roller to ensure a smooth finish, apply a wood primer that will seal the knots and block stains. Use a 25mm angled brush to apply the primer in the corners. Leave to dry.

3. Once dry, decant the paint into a mini roller paint tray. Paint the furniture in your chosen base colour using the 25mm angled brush to paint the edges and any grooves, and blend over the wet edge with a mini foam roller. Leave to dry. Add a second coat for durability.

4. Once dry, put the drawers back into the chest before proceeding. Ensure only one drawer is open at a time so the furniture does not tip.

TOP TIP

```
Insert the knobs on the reverse
of the drawer front, so the slim
thread of the screw is pointing
towards you so you can open and
close the drawer, while painting
the drawer front.
```

5. To add the rectangular checkerboard pattern to your drawer fronts, measure the width of your drawer. Decide roughly how many checkerboards you would like (an odd number is recommended). For example, if you drawer front is 700mm across and your would like 9 checkerboards, each rectangle will be 77.7mm across.

6. Measure across from left to right, add a small pencil mark at each point. Use a laser level to project a vertical beam through this point and apply a low-tac masking tape to alternating rectangles – a taped checkerboard will start to appear.

7. Once taped, seal the edges of the tape by firmly smoothing it down with your finger and paint the outline of your shape in the base colour. This will give you the crispest paint line with no puckering or splatters of your contrast colour. Leave to dry.

8. Now it's finally time to add the contrast paint. Paint alternate rectangles as you work along each drawer front. To avoid brush marks, fill in your piece with a mini foam roller. However, if the shape is too small for a roller, fill in with a brush, painting in one direction and overlapping your brush strokes so it dries flat.

9. Remove the tape when wet, gently pulling it back on itself at a 45-degree angle so you don't remove the base colour. Take your time.

10. If the furniture is placed in a high-traffic area of the house, apply a clear finishing wax with a waxing brush to seal the wood and provide additional durability, then admire your unique one-off item!

TOP TIP

```
Consider upgrading the drawer
knobs to elevate your piece
even further.
```

HOW TO TRANSFORM A PHOTO FRAME WITH GOLD LEAF

Gold leaf can add a touch of luxe to any item and is a seriously satisfying (if slightly messy) way of upcycling furniture or small thrifted knick-knacks. As gold leaf is a more expensive finish than say, paint, choose a smaller item to work with. It works on many materials — wood, stone, metals — and you can also try copper and pewter finishes if you want a little less bling. I recommend you purchase a gold leaf starter pack from an arts and craft store or online as these will include all the tools and materials required: the gold leaf sheets, adhesive, sealer, brush and gloves.

TOOLBOX
```
Clean cloth
Dust brush
Gold-leaf
  adhesive - will
  come with its
  own brush
Gloves, if using
Gold-leaf sheets
Soft cotton cloth
Sealant/varnish
Masking tape, if
  using
```

TROUBLESHOOTING
The gold leaf sheets have a paper backing and it is important to leave these on.

1. Take your photo frame apart by unclipping and removing the board and glass/Perspex. Clean the frame surface you are about to gild, then dry thoroughly. If you are only applying gold leaf to a small section, use masking tape to create a straight boundary line.

2. Brush the adhesive in a thin layer onto the area you want to cover, then leave for 15–30 minutes for it to turn tacky – the perfect opportunity to grab a coffee.

3. If the glue has turned from white to transparent, it is now workable. With clean dry hands (or wearing gloves, if included in your kit) lift the gold leaf sheets one at a time and lay them onto the adhesive with the paper side up.

4. Gently press down evenly over the back of the paper, then peel off the paper backing, leaving the gold leaf layer on the surface. Do not worry if there are creases or wrinkles as these will soon be buffed into oblivion.

5. Using a soft cotton cloth, rub the gilded surface to remove the small excess flakes, until a smooth surface appears.

6. If you have gaps in the gold, brush over with a small amount of adhesive and repeat steps 3 to 5 until you have a perfect finish.

7. Leave your item to dry fully for up to 3 days. Small projects will dry more quickly. This will vary dependent on the size and area of your gold leafing.

8. Using a clean brush, apply the sealant/varnish over the gold leaf. Assuming you are using imitation gold leaf, this is essential to avoid tarnishing.

HOW TO MAKE BOBBIN PICTURE FRAMES

QUICK & QUIET

Displaying photographs and posters in frames brings a personal touch to your home. Bobbin frames are made from 'bobbin balls' which are wooden beads that have been sliced in half, and they are the perfect way to update old frames or to give that existing mirror a fun transformation. This mindful craft is quick to execute and super satisfying, so put the kettle on, download a podcast and find a calm space to work.

TOOLBOX

```
30 x 40cm photo
  frame
15mm bobbin balls
Hot glue gun
  or wood glue/
  adhesive
Ruler or spirit
  level
Wood primer,
  if using
Spray paint or
  topcoat paint,
  if using
```

TROUBLESHOOTING

- For frames that aren't so easily handled, a hot-glue gun will give you a firm(ish) fix and the frame will dry in seconds, ready for painting.
- For larger bobbin projects, use a wood adhesive or 'no nails' product. This has a longer drying time but will provide a firmer fix for your design.

1. Lie the frame on the table and experiment with the spacing of the bobbin balls. You can position them flush in line with the edge of the frame, or slightly off-centre to give the edges of the frame a scalloped shape.

2. Apply a small bead of glue to the flat back of the bobbin and press firmly onto the photo frame.

3. Repeat with more bobbins to create a straight line along all the edges of the frame. A ruler or a spirit level can be very useful for keeping the lines straight. If using wood adhesive, leave to cure overnight.

4. To complete the frame, finish with your paint of choice or leave the bobbins 'raw' and natural. If painting, you can add a thin layer of wood primer to give you a super durable finish, but this is optional (check if you have any leftover from a previous DIY project). Using a spray paint will give you a flawless finish and make it easier to cover all the bumps and grooves. However, you could also use paint leftover from decorating, which would complement the existing colours of your home. Leave the paint to dry.

5. Add your favourite pictures to the frame and then find the perfect place in the house to display it. See how to design a gallery wall on page 106.

TOP TIP

Bobbin balls are available in many different sizes. I have worked with 15mm balls and scaled up to a 30mm ball for a chunkier look on larger print frames or mirrors. Get a ruler out and see what diameter works for you (they are also available as 12mm and 10mm).

UPCYCLE IT

HOW TO MAKEOVER IKEA FURNITURE

The 'IKEA hack' has soared in popularity in recent years as people look for ways to reinvent their existing furniture on a budget. Social media is inundated with images and videos of classic IKEA items (KALLAX, BILLY, PAX, MALM, to name four of the most popular models) which have been elevated from simple white melamine to a painted storage dream.

To upcycle IKEA furniture effectively, it is important to understand its construction. Many items are made from melamine particleboard that has been wrapped in a vinyl wood veneer, with a sheen that can be cleaned easily. This makes it weaker than solid wood furniture and harder to achieve a secure fix with paint. Therefore, some special preparation is needed to ensure your paint finish does not peel or scratch off easily. These instructions are suitable for the wood-veneered IKEA models listed above.

TOOLBOX
```
120-grit
  sandpaper
Clean, damp cloth
Paint primer
Paint tray
Mini foam roller
25mm paintbrush
Topcoat paint
Sealant, if using
```

TROUBLESHOOTING
```
If you can, paint the item before it is built. However,
if the item has already been assembled, you may wish
to semi-dismantle it to improve the quality of your
paint finish.
```

1. Using 120-grit sandpaper, work up and down the long length of the panels in the same direction. Every surface you intend to paint must be thoroughly sanded to provide a key for the primer and paint to stick to.

2. Remove the dust and use a lightly damp cloth to clean the surface. Leave to dry.

3. Pour some primer paint into a roller tray and, using a small foam roller, add a layer of primer to the furniture panels, then leave to dry. If your furniture is assembled, paint into the corners with a 25mm paintbrush. Brands such as Zinsser and Valspar have primer products that are specifically formulated to cover melamine and veneered surfaces.

4 After the first coat of primer has dried, lightly sand the piece again and clean with a damp cloth. Then add a second coat of primer. A second coat is advised for pieces that will receive heavy use but, if not necessary, proceed to the topcoat.

5 Your topcoat choice is down to you (see page 120 for guidance), but I recommend an eggshell or satin wood paint that is more durable than an emulsion or chalk finish. Pour the paint into a roller tray and apply using a foam roller in a thin layer for the best finish. The most durable finish consists of several thin layers, rather than one thick one which can chip easily. Leave to dry for a minimum of 2 hours.

6 To seal or not to seal, that is the question. If you have used a water-based paint, adding a water-based clear sealant to the furniture can help prolong its lifespan. However, it can also change the colour and texture of your paint finish. I advise you test it first by painting an offcut in your topcoat and add the sealant to check that you are happy with the finish. If so, use a small foam roller to give your furniture two even coats of sealant, leaving a minimum of 2 hours between coats. If you have used an oil-based paint, brushing clear furniture wax over the surface can provide extra durability.

7 Avoid using the item for up to 72 hours to allow the paint to fully cure and harden.

> **TOP TIP**
> Panelling can be added to elevate the piece further. Try cladding the sides in tongue and groove or add moulding to the doors. Follow the guide in the 'Panel It' chapter if you want to try this. You can also add feet to lift the piece off the ground or change the handles.

FINAL THOUGHTS

And that, my friends, brings us to the end of the book. But rest assured, our DIY journey does not end here, as we all continue to learn, try, succeed, occasionally bodge and fill it... and try again.

DIY and home improvements are part of the continuous cycle of life. As the years go by, the wear and tear will return again! A paint colour will fall out of favour, a child will declare that they no longer like unicorns/tractors, a dog will chew the furniture, the silicone will go mouldy, and a mysterious stain will appear on your walls, it just will! And so the journey starts again.

But that is life, and our homes are there to be lived in and enjoyed. It's important to adapt them to our ever-changing needs and to take pride in all the evolutions along the way. Pick a colour because you love it. And be even prouder if you prepped and painted it. But be patient with yourself and your personal DIY learning curve. You might find power tools tricky to negotiate but be an absolute wallpapering wizard. You might struggle to put up a shelf but smash panelling in a day. Do not give up. Allow yourself time and, if in doubt, call in friends or family for advice and assistance and to make it a sociable thing!

Also, promise me one very important thing: before you get pulled in a different direction or start a new task, sit back and look at your work once you are finished, and feel/relish that sense of accomplishment.

You Nailed It!